Thatcher's Reign

A Bad Case
of the Blues

Thatcher's Reign

A Bad Case of the Blues

Melanie McFadyean and Margaret Renn

Chatto & Windus · The Hogarth Press London

Published in 1984 by
Chatto & Windus · The Hogarth Press
40 William IV Street
London WC2N 4DF

British Library Cataloguing in
Publication Data

McFadyean, Melanie
Thatcher's Reign.
1. Great Britain—Politics and government
—1979–
I. Title II. Renn, Margaret
354.4107'2'09 JN231

ISBN 0-7011-2857-7

Printed in Great Britain by Butler & Tanner Ltd

Contents

Acknowledgements

Our thanks to the Child Poverty Action Group; CND; Incomes Data Report; the Low Pay Unit; Labour Research; the Royal College of Nursing; Shelter; the London Housing Aid Centre (SHAC); Tony Bunyan of the GLC Police Committee Support Unit; Paul Gordon of the Runnymede Trust; David Pallister; Dennis Skinner MP; and Paul Foot whose column in the *Daily Mirror* has covered the first five years of Margaret Thatcher's reign. And a special thank you to Elana Dallas.

We would also like to acknowledge BBC Television and Radio; the *Daily Mirror; Daily Mail; Daily Express; Daily Telegraph; Economist;* Granada Television; *Guardian;* the London *Evening News* and *Evening Standard;* London Weekend Television; *News of the World; New Statesman; Reader's Digest; Sunday Times; Sunday Telegraph; Sunday Express; Sunday People;* Thames Television; *Time Out* and *The Times.*Extracts from *Hansard* are reproduced with permission of the controller of HMSO.

We thank the following for permission to reproduce photographs: *Basingstoke Gazette,* page 27; Camera Press, pages 7, 11, 67, 86; Elisabeth Photo Library, page 76; Peter Kennard, page 113; Keystone Press Agency, pages 8, 31, 54, 98, 117, 124; Bob Light and John Houston, page 95; Network, pages 24, 62; Popperfoto, pages 11, 39, 47, 58, 73, 78, 83, 89, 109, 114, 119, 120, 127; Syndication International, pages 34, 123. Thanks to Lucke and Flaw, and Gill Wing, for the teapot on page 25 (photo by Darryl Williams).

Margaret and Muriel Roberts

'I suppose I was about 20, and a crowd of us had been to a village hop and came back to make midnight cups of coffee. I was in the kitchen helping to dish up and having a fierce argument with one of the boys in the crowd when someone else interrupted to say: "Of course, Margaret, you will go in for politics won't you?" I stopped dead. Suddenly it was crystallised for me. I knew.' (*Daily Express*, 17.4.61)

Curriculum Vitae

13.10.25   Margaret Hilda Roberts born in Grantham, Lincolnshire
Father: Alfred Roberts, grocer, one time JP and Mayor of Grantham
Mother: Beatrice, former seamstress
One older sister: Muriel

1936   Attends Grantham Girls' School; specialises in sciences and becomes Head Girl.

1943   Reads Chemistry at Somerville College, Oxford.

1945   Canvasses for Tory candidate Quintin Hogg (Lord Hailsham).

Labour wins the general election.

1946   First woman President of the Oxford University Conservative Association.

1947   Works as research chemist at British Xylonite, Essex.

1948   Represents Oxford University Graduate Association at Tory Party Conference.

'I do take some small consolation that there is only one small vowel sound between ruin and run. The small vowel sound is "I".'
(*Financial Times*, 17.9.75)

9

'You know how it is, if your
hair looks awful you feel
awful.' (*Daily Mail*, 7.7.65)

Selected as Tory candidate for Dartford, Kent.

1950   Works for J. Lyons, investigating new fillings for Swiss rolls and methods for preserving the foamy quality of ice cream.

Meets Denis Thatcher.

Fails to win Dartford seat; Labour wins general election.

1951   In her spare time, studies Law.

Marries Denis Thatcher.

Fails to win Dartford seat for the second time; Tories win the general election.

1953   The twins – Mark and Carol – are born in August. Margaret passes her Bar exams in December.

1954   Called to the Bar; becomes full-time tax barrister.

1959   Selected as Tory candidate for Finchley.

Becomes MP for Finchley; Tories win the general election.

1960   Makes maiden speech on Public Bodies (Admission to Meetings) Bill. The Bill is passed.

1961   Joint Parliamentary Secretary for Pensions and National Insurance.

1964   Labour wins general election.

'My hats seem to incense some people.' (*Daily Mail*, 8.2.72)

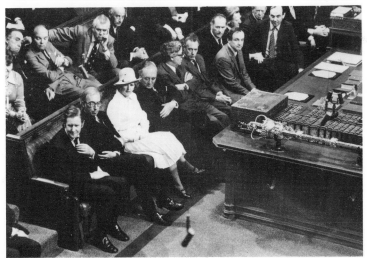

'I like to be made a fuss of by a lot of chaps.' (*Daily Mirror*, 14.2.75.)

'I don't want to give my life over entirely to politics. I don't think I'd have the ability and I'd never be given the chance.' (*Sunday Times*, 5.3.67)

1965   Spokeswoman for Housing and Land.

1966   Spokeswoman for the Treasury.

1967   Shadow Cabinet spokeswoman for Power.

1968   Shadow Minister for Transport.

1969   Shadow Minister for Education.

'[In Number 10] I'm going to have furniture I like ... because I intend to be there a long, long time.' (BBC Radio 1, 20.11.77)

1970   Tories win the general election; Mrs Thatcher becomes Secretary of State for Education.

1974   Labour wins general election in February.

Labour increases its majority in the October election; Tory Party leadership battle begins.

1975   Becomes leader of the Tory Party.

'I owe a great deal to the Church for everything in which I believe. I am very glad that I was brought up strictly ... I was a very serious child ... There was not a lot of fun and sparkle in my life.' (*Daily Telegraph*, 7.6.80)

1976   Harold Wilson resigns as Prime Minister; James Callaghan takes over.

1979   Tories win general election in May. Margaret Thatcher becomes Prime Minister.

1983   Tories win general election; Thatcher enters second term of office.

That's the Way the Money Goes – Wealth and Poverty

'This business of the working class is on its way out I think. After all, aren't I working class? I work jolly hard, I can tell you.' (*Evening News*, London, 5.10.69)

While inspecting carpets in a factory in Halifax in 1978, Mrs Thatcher commented on how lovely they were. A woman worker said, *'But they're very expensive for us working people.'* Mrs Thatcher replied:

'We're all working people and they're very expensive for us all.' (*Guardian*, 23.3.78)

In 1951 Margaret Roberts married Denis Thatcher, managing director of his family's firm.

'I do not have to worry about money.' (*Guardian*, 23.3.62)

In 1965 Denis Thatcher sold his company for a figure estimated to be £560,000. He then became a director of Burmah Oil. The children went to public schools.

'The charm of Britain has always been the ease with which one can move into the middle class.' (*Evening Standard*, London, 24.10.74)

'Some say I preach merely the homilies of house-keeping or the parables of the parlour. But I do not repent. Those parables would have saved many a financier from failure and many a country from crisis.' (Lord Mayor's Banquet, 15.11.82)

DID YOU KNOW? ☞

'It is expensive to be in politics; one has to be mobile, one has to be well groomed, and one has to entertain.' (*Guardian*, 23.3.62)

'No one would remember the Good Samaritan if he had only had good intentions. He had money as well.' (*The Times*, 12.2.80)

In 1975 Denis Thatcher retired from Burmah Oil, with a yearly pension of £5,000, but he continued to work on the boards of three companies associated with Burmah Oil.

'I am really very normal. I'm just a perfectly ordinary person.' (*Sunday Express*, 16.1.77)

'I'm not as posh as I sound. I'm not grand at all.' (*Daily Mirror*, 7.2.77)

When Margaret Thatcher became leader of the Conservative Party she said:

'There are too few rich and too few profits.' (*Daily Telegraph*, 12.6.75)

She promised to do something about it.

'Free enterprise has enabled the creative and acquisitive urges of man to be given expression in a way which benefits all members of society. Let free enterprise fight back now, not for itself but for all those who believe in freedom.' (Speech, Free Enterprise Day Luncheon, 1.7.75)

In his first budget, Geoffrey Howe swept away dividend control – the limit that could be paid to shareholders in any one year. In 1978, personal shareholders were paid £2,950 million. In the first full year after dividend control was lifted, they were paid £4,650 million – a rise of 58%. In the same period profits went up by 9.4%.

'Today it seems as if people are made to feel guilty about being well off. But Christ did not condemn riches as such, only the way in which they were used and those who put their trust in them.' (Speech from the pulpit of St Lawrence Jewry, 30.3.78)

Between 1979 and 1982 the salaries of the top 28 company directors in Britain went up from an average of £98,000 a year to £191,000.

'We need to create a mood where it is everywhere thought morally right for as many people as possible to acquire capital.' (Speech, Conservative Political Centre, 6.7.79)

'Pennies don't fall from heaven, they have to be earned here on earth.' (Lord Mayor's Banquet, 13.11.79)

On 16 March 1984 the *Financial Times* share index hit an all time high of 894.7. Two years previously it had stood at 518.1. In two years the wealth of shareholders had increased by 73%. One Conservative MP, Sally Oppenheim, said: *'It is about time we removed the scales from our eyes, abandoned the humbug and admitted that the pursuit of self-interest is not only what each of us practises but is also beneficial for the rest of us.'* (Speech, National TV Rental Association, 10.6.80)

Mrs. Thatcher has also pledged:

'We shall protect the poor and those in most need of help.' (*Guardian*, 9.3.84)

◄ PROMISES, PROMISES

'We have a duty to the most vulnerable members of our society, many of whom have contributed to the heritage we now enjoy.' (Manifesto, 1983)

In 1979 there were 4.4 million people, including pensioners, living on means-tested supplementary benefit. This number had risen to 7.3 million in 1983, an increase of 72%.

'The number on supplementary benefits has increased largely due to the number of unemployed. They are able to get sufficient for their needs.' (*Hansard*, 12.4.83)

'I said at the start I shall get things right in the end, and I shall.' (*Daily Express*, 13.8.80)

When asked about the number of people living on the breadline Margaret Thatcher replied:

'It all depends on what you mean by the breadline.' (*Hansard*, 1.11.83)

DID YOU KNOW? ☛ 'There is no government definition of poverty. There are some seven million people that live in families that are supported by supplementary benefits. The fact remains that people living in need are fully and properly provided for.' (*Hansard*, 22.12.83)

When Labour was in power she said:

'We will not tolerate Britain becoming the poor relation of Europe.' (*Sunday People*, 3.6.79) 'We have changed places with Italy. It is to Britain that the journalists now come, following the scent of economic and political decay.' (*Sunday Telegraph*, 18.3.75)

In 1984 an EEC survey showed that 29 out of 33 British regions are below the Community average in terms of economic recovery and output.

'I do not believe it is in the character of the British people to begrudge the lion's share to those who have genuinely played the lion's part. They are ready to recognise that those who create the wealth – and I mean not only material but intellectual wealth – enrich the whole nation.' (*Evening News*, London, 23.9.74)

One a Minute – Unemployment

'I think it's terrible if a person who wants to work can't find a job. You have no self-respect, you haven't got the respect of your family if, somehow, you can't earn yourself a living and them a living too.' (Party Political Broadcast, 4.5.77)

In May 1977, 1.3 million people were unemployed. In March 1984, after nearly five years of Thatcher's reign, the figure was 3.1 million.

In Opposition Margaret Thatcher hammered away at Labour's record:

'Judged by performance, which is the only test by which to judge any government, the Labour Party has now become the national party of unemployment.' (*Hansard*, 20.1.76)

'Whatever excuses the Prime Minister [James Callaghan] may give, he cannot run away from the fact that our policies did not produce unemployment as his have. He will go down in history as the Prime Minister for Unemployment.' (*The Times*, 25.1.78)

'One person has joined the dole queue every four minutes of Labour rule.' (Speech, Darlington, 23.4.79)

As of March 1984, one person had joined the dole queue

'Unemployment is one of the great unsolved mysteries of our time.' (Speech, *Guardian* Young Businessman of the Year Award, 11.3.82)

17

every 1½ minutes of Tory rule; 1,048 jobs had been lost every day.

In office, her tone changes:

WISHFUL THINKING ☛ **'I do hope to goodness that the jobless total never gets to two and a half million but there will be no change in our economic policies because they are absolutely right.'** (*Daily Mirror*, 28.8.80)
Unemployment was 1,846,100.

'If we are not careful, a lot of industry will not be around when the revival comes.' (Terence Beckett, Director of the Confederation of British Industry, 11.11.80)

'It's like the begininning stages of when you take a medicine. For a time you are suffering both from the illness and from the medicine.' (German TV, 11.80)
Unemployment goes up to 2,016,000.

'There is real hope that a year from now things will be looking distinctly brighter.' (*Conservative News*, 12.80)
Unemployment goes up to 2,099,900.

'Of course I am deeply concerned about the plight of the unemployed and those businesses which are suffering severely. We shall do everything we can to help them. What we cannot do is change our essential strategy.' (*News of the World*, 4.1.81)
Unemployment goes up to 2,271,100.

'There are signs that the recession is coming to an end.' (Speech, Bombay, India, 17.4.81)
Unemployment goes up to 2,372,700.

'Unless the stock markets have got it very wrong, we are in for a dramatic recovery in the profitability of British industry in the months ahead.' (Speech, Scottish Conservatives, 8.5.81)

Unemployment goes up to 2,407,400.

'We are now beginning to win through.' (Speech, CBI dinner, 16.6.81)
Unemployment goes down to 2,395,200.

'I think we are through the worst of the recession.' (Speech, Glasgow, 3.9.81)
Unemployment goes up again, to 2,748,600.

'I believe we can begin to see the first signs of recovery in the UK.' (Lord Mayor's Banquet, 16.11.81)
Unemployment goes up to 2,769,500.

'I think we are through the worst.' (New Year message, 2.1.82)
Unemployment goes up to 2,896,300.

The Thatcher strategy remains unaffected by rising unemployment. Jobs must be sacrificed to bring down prices.

'Everyone would accept we do everything possible to alleviate unemployment, particularly among young people. We are not prepared to print money to do it.' (*Hansard*, 16.6.80)

'In the early stages bringing down inflation does mean that you have increasing unemployment and I don't know any other way of doing it.' (*Time*, 2.81)

Mrs Thatcher boasts of her success:

'By improved technology and efficiency we are producing the same output, with 1.7 million fewer in the workforce.' (*Hansard*, 31.3.84)

'One in eight of our people is unemployed – far, far too many – but seven out of eight are in fact working.' (*Daily Telegraph*, 10.12.83)

'There is no magic about what I am doing. None at all. If we carry on with it long enough it will work. It works, it works, it works. The alternatives will not.' (*News of the World*, 20.9.81)

Her strategy depends on cutting inflation and boosting productivity. The quickest way to boost productivity figures is to cut the workforce, so that fewer people do more work.

'I believe that in stopping over-manning and restrictive practices we will not increase unemployment, but decrease it.' (*Daily Mail*, 3.5.80)

But within two years she was claiming:

'We've taken the over-manning and hidden unemployment out of industry and it's come onto the unemployment register. But at least we've got an efficient industry from which to expand.' (Thames Television, 18.2.82)

Who is to blame for rising unemployment?

'We all hate unemployment, but we all remember that it was the previous government who increased it so much.' (*Hansard*, 19.7.79)

In November 1982, she still blamed her predecessors:

'A major cause is the failure of the Right Honourable gentleman [James Callaghan] and his Right Honourable friends to attack the roots of unemployment when they were in office.' (*Hansard*, 3.11.82)

She also blames school-leavers:

'Unemployment will rise, of course it will, because of the increasing number of school-leavers and because there is a substantial increase in the numbers in the labour force. That

'What woman welcomes the turmoil of moving house? Who wants to separate herself from old friends and neighbours to set about finding new schools for the children and discovering by experiment who is the best local butcher?' (Speech, Swansea, 20.7.80)

is because fewer people are retiring and there are more school-leavers.' (*Hansard*, 24.6.81)

And their lack of skills:

'One of the saddest features of modern-day Britain is not simply that we have school-leavers for whom there are few openings, but that we have job-seekers with so few marketable skills to offer potential employers.' (*Reader's Digest*, 1.84)

And their high wages:

'We would have more young people employed if somehow people who are responsible for negotiating wages had not insisted on much higher wages for young people. This has meant that a lot of firms have not been able to take them on.' (BBC Radio 4, 4.1.81)

It's not only young people who are pricing themselves out of jobs:

'If people would work for the amount of money that they are receiving in unemployed pay and social security in the public sector, the extra we would have to find would be the materials, the supervision and the premises. But to suggest to them that they work for that – I am afraid they just simply would not.' (*Sunday Telegraph*, 14.2.82)

And there are women who expect to have a job:

'There are more women looking for work. We have to create more jobs just to stop unemployment getting worse.' (*News of the World*, 4.1.81)

'Helmut Schmidt ... sent nearly half a million *gastarbeiter* [immigrant workers] home, which we couldn't do, and he's got compulsory conscription which takes a whole year of young people off the unemployment register. So, yes, I get on extremely well with Helmut Schmidt. My policies and his were the same.' (BBC Radio 4, 30.3.83)

In 1980, the rules of the Employment Transfer Scheme changed. If you did 'get on your bike' there was less chance of getting removal expenses. The number of people receiving assistance under the scheme dropped from 9,785 in 1979–80 to 5,668 in 1980–81, and has continued to fall.

And all those who are unwilling to 'get on their bikes':

'People are reluctant to move, even a comparatively small distance, to take new jobs. There must be some mobility of labour. If people today are not willing to move as their fathers did, the economy cannot thrive.' (Speech, Welsh Conservatives, 20.7.80)

Could the world recession be the cause?

'It is a fact that 1980 was the year of the worst world recession since the 1930s. No British government has had to face anything quite as bad as this for nearly fifty years. Every industrial country has suffered – and in every one of them unemployment has risen sharply. Certainly, Britain has suffered worse than most.' (*News of the World*, 4.1.81)

Perhaps the price of oil is the problem?

'When I first went into Downing Street as Prime Minister, oil cost $14 a barrel. Now it is about $35 a barrel. That reduced the amount of money available to buy other things. So inevitably the demand for other things fell and so unemployment rose.' (Speech, Department of Energy Schools Competition winners, 27.1.82)

'Labour's favourite but totally false excuse is that their appalling record is all due to the oil crisis and the world economic recession.' (Manifesto, 1979)

So one shouldn't blame oil prices and the world recession for the rise in unemployment?

U-TURN ☛ *'We did not disguise the fact that putting Britain right would be an extremely difficult task. The second sharp oil* *increase and the deepest world recession since the 1930s have made these difficulties worse.'* (Manifesto, 1983)

Perhaps, then, foreigners are to blame:

'The Japanese and Germans are taking our business and our jobs.' (*Daily Telegraph*, 28.8.80)

'If more of our people bought more of the produce of our industries there would be more employment in this country.' (*Hansard*, 14.12.81)

And strikers:

'Some people have been striking themselves out of jobs.' (*Hansard*, 7.5.81)

And trade unionists:

'The trade unions are destroying the very jobs which they claim to defend.' (*Hansard*, 22.6.83)

And, when all else fails:

'It has been usual for there to be a sharp increase in unemployment between December and January because of the weather.' (*Hansard*, 17.12.81)

Everything, it seems, causes unemployment except her own policies. Not that she doesn't sympathise with the un-employed:

'I couldn't live without work. That's what makes me so sympathetic towards those people who are unemployed. I don't know how they live without working.' (*News of the World*, 4.5.80)

'Pessimists say that we can never solve unemployment. They are wrong and I intend to prove it.' (Norman Tebbit, 7.8.82)

'The prospect of a sharp fall in unemployment is, to say the least, very poor.' (Norman Tebbit, 9.8.82)

The number of people out of work for over a year reached 1,188,000 in February 1984, nearly the same as the total number of people unemployed when Mrs Thatcher took office.

'A tragedy, the human tragedy of unemployment, especially prolonged unemployment, is an evil, and high levels of unemployment a tragic waste of human and material resources.' (*Hansard*, 2.6.81)

But:

'It is easy to speak about the tragedy of unemployment. We have to seek ways of alleviating it and creating genuine wealth and genuine jobs for Britain.' (*Hansard*, 22.6.83)

The official unemployment figure for March 1984 stood at 3,142,775. However, people who can't claim benefits are no longer included in the statistics, nor are men aged over 60, and the Government's Youth Training Scheme has temporarily removed another 200,000 from the register. The real unemployment figure is over four million.

In Opposition, Margaret Thatcher was outraged when unemployment reached 1.3 million:

'Sometimes I've heard it said that Conservatives have been associated with unemployment. That's absolutely wrong. We'd have been drummed out of office if we'd had this level of unemployment.' (Party Political Broadcast, 4.5.77)

'Yesterday's exaggeration is today's understatement.'
(*Observer*, 7.9.75)

Go-Getters and Risk-Takers – Small Businesses

For the last four years we in the Conservative Party have been shouting ourselves hoarse about the number of jobs being lost as small businesses have had to close down in their thousands – victims of Labour's taxation and bureaucracy.' (Speech, Putney, 17.2.78)

'We will need a host of small businesses run by talented young people who are prepared to work night and day in return for big rewards if they succeed.' (Speech, Food and Drink Industries Council, 31.3.78)

They will need help:

'What are the do's and don'ts for more genuine jobs and real prosperity? Don't tax profits so much that people won't take risks. You can't expect them to risk almost everything they've got to set up in business if they bear all the losses and the government takes nearly all the gains. Don't envy the success of others – applaud it.' (Speech, Scottish Young Conservatives, 1.9.78)

This is how jobs will be created:

'Jobs grow not out of windy promises and implausible targets. They spring from creative individual effort, com-

'I will not change just to court popularity.' (Speech, Conservative Party Conference, 16.10.81)

'There will be three years of realism – four years, five years, I hope ten years of opportunity. I don't think there will be three years of unparalleled austerity.' (*Daily Telegraph*, 25.2.80)

bined with high skill and hard work. Give one man the chance, the incentives, to start up on his own and you soon give a dozen people the chance to work with him. Today's big business is yesterday's small business.' (Speech, Scotland, 25.5.79)

But a spokesman for the Association of Independent Businesses (representing 30,000 small businesses), told the *Daily Telegraph*: '*It is significant that when small businessmen get together they tend today to emphasise how few they employ to achieve their targets, rather than how many*' (4.5.84).

VITAL STATISTIC ☛ In the last five years there have been a record 80,000 bankruptcies and liquidations – 20,000 of them in 1983.

In August 1981 Margaret Thatcher went to the Norplan factory in Norwich. '**Marvellous**,' she said. In October 1982, the receiver was called in.

In 1980 Posidata opened their computer factory in Basingstoke. '**Our task is to create the financial climate and the business climate in which you can start to grow**,' said Mrs Thatcher. In January 1983, 15 of the 60 workers were made redundant and 13 more were leaving, or were under notice.

In March 1980 Mrs Thatcher visited the shipyard of Austin and Pickersgill, in Sunderland, returning in March 1982 to launch a new ship (the workers boycotted this visit). In February 1983, 300 redundancies were announced.

In June 1981, it was the turn of Airfoil Developments, Warminster. '**This company is an advertisement for private enterprise**,' Mrs Thatcher told them. The company closed down in May 1983.

In 1979 Mrs Thatcher visited HH Electronics, Cambridge. It was thriving, with 350 workers employed at the plant. In 1984, the receivers were called in. She had said on her visit:

'A wonderful success story that ought to be repeated.'
(*Daily Mirror*, 2.2.84)

'I am afraid some things will get worse before they get better. We did not promise you instant sunshine.'
(Party political broadcast, 12.3.80)

Prime Cuts –

Tax

'Self-reliance has been sneered at as if it were an absurd suburban pretension. Thrift has been denigrated as if it were greed … More than 50 years ago Bernard Shaw sent a shiver down the spine of England in his play *Heartbreak House* with its version of this country as an unnavigable ship manned by a gambling crew – heading through wild seas straight for the rocks. It might have been expressly written with Socialist Britain in mind.' (*Sunday Express*, 16.3.75)

'We have to cut taxes: the tax on earnings, the tax on savings, the tax on talent.' (Party Political Broadcast, 2.4.79)

'Taxes must and taxes will come down.' (Speech, Finchley, 11.4.79)

In spite of Margaret Thatcher's election promises, in 1984 all but the top earners were paying more tax.

'We will cut taxes so that people can look after themselves and their families, so they can build for their own future.' (Speech, Conservative Central Council, 24.3.79)

But it would take a tax cut of 9p in the pound to bring the tax burden down to what it was in 1978–9 for a couple on average earnings. For a couple on three-quarters of average earnings it would take a cut of 11½p in the pound.

Under the previous Tory Government the standard rate of income tax had been cut to 30p in the pound.

'We will hope, obviously, to do better than that. Unless someone does that, does it positively and with determination and, I might even say, with a passionate belief that it has to be done, then I see no hope and I see no change from perpetual decline.' (Press conference, 23.4.79)

'To pay for tax cuts, curb inflation and give industry the room to expand we shall have to reduce the State's take of what the nation earns.' (Speech, Conservative Central Council, 24.3.79)

To pay for tax cuts, public spending must be cut. Welfare services have indeed been cut – but not taxes. Unless, that is, you earn more than £18,000 a year. If you earn less than this, any tax cuts you enjoy will have to be paid for:

'Considerable reductions in the lower rates of tax on incomes are just as urgent. We all need incentives. But here the implications for the public revenues are formidable indeed. In part, the loss of revenue can be recouped – and may have to be recouped – by higher rates on spending.' (Speech, Finance Houses Association, 25.1.79)

In the Tories first budget in 1979, the lowest rate of tax was cut from 33p to 30p in the pound. But the tax on spending – VAT – went up from 8% to 15%.

'The switch from direct to indirect taxation in the budget increases freedom of choice.' (Speech, Conservative Political Centre, 6.7.79)

The poorer you are, the more you pay in indirect taxes such as VAT. The lowest income group pay more than 25% of their income in indirect tax; the highest earners pay only 16%.

'Most people on low wages spend most of their money on necessities – and necessities just don't attract VAT. It's better to give the person the choice on what they spend it on

'But I say to you;
The ship sails East
The ship sails West,
Whatever the wind that blows,
'Tis the set of the sail
And not the gale,
That determines the way she goes.' (Speech, Engineering Employers' Federation, 23.2.82)

'Our country is weathering stormy waters. We may have different ideas on how to navigate them, but we sail the same ocean in the same ship.' (Conservative Party Conference, 17.10.81)

than to take it away from them and give them no choice at all.' (Thames Television, 24.4.79)

Mrs Thatcher spelt out what she meant by 'necessities':

'There's no VAT on food; there's no VAT on fuel; no VAT on public transport, none on housing, no VAT on children's clothes or shoes.' (Ibid.)

But there is VAT on all household goods, such as toilet rolls, washing-up liquid and soap, and on adults' clothes, telephone bills, household furniture and repairs. In the 1984 budget, VAT was extended to take-away food.

VAT isn't graded like income tax; families living on supplementary benefit pay at the same rate as the country's highest-paid earners.

Mrs Thatcher claimed:

'Taking account of the income tax reductions as well as the indirect tax increase, a family on average earnings will be better off over the period between the budget and the end of the financial year. They will be paying about £2.75 a week more for what they buy because VAT has gone up. But they will have about £4 a week more to spend because of income tax reductions.' (Speech, Conservative Political Centre, 6.7.79)

But they don't have £4 a week more to spend, only £1.25 after allowing for increases in VAT.

There were National Insurance contribution increases to come too. Between 1979 and 1984 contributions increased from 6.5% to 9% of income. Mrs Thatcher attacked the Labour Government for similar manoeuvres:

'Don't be taken in. The effect of reducing the rate of tax is to

reduce people's tax bills by £1.73 at most. Very welcome. But remember that in the same month of April, National Insurance contributions are going up. Some will pay 60p a week more. Others up to £1.75 a week more – enough to wipe out that tax relief. This government takes with one hand what it gives with the other.' (Speech, Putney, 17.2.78)

'Economics are the method; the object is to change the soul.' (*Sunday Times*, 3.5.81)

But ...

'A family, an average family, on average earnings, is doing better on taxation now than under the last Labour government ... if you take it on tax alone. What my opponents do is say, "Well, don't just take the tax, add those National Insurance contributions which you have to pay." But may I point out that they are not a tax, they are an insurance contribution which, if you don't pay, you don't get the benefits.' (London Weekend Television, 15.1.84)

WISHFUL THINKING

In March 1984, Nigel Lawson, Chancellor of the Exchequer, published a Government Green Paper on public expenditure and taxation. It explains the tax burden as '*Taxes plus Rates and National Insurance contributions as a percentage of Gross Domestic Product*' (what the nation produces each year) and says, '*Taxes and Rates, plus National Insurance contributions, were some 29% of Gross Domestic Product in 1963–4, rose to 34% in 1978–9 and 38% by 1984*'.

'The level of taxation is far too high on middle management.' (BBC Radio 4, 17.7.75)

The Prime Minister's deepest sympathies lie with management:

'We must restore the motivation, morale and authority of

management. **No group is more important, and yet none
has been so put through the mangle and flattened between
the rollers of penally progressive taxation and discrimina-
tory incomes policy. And it is not even as though British
management was well remunerated at the start.'** (Speech,
Engineering Employers Federation, 21.2.78)

Managers have been driven to desperate measures:

**'Men and women who have built a business, giving work
and satisfaction to their fellow citizens, go from our shores
to the sterile refuge of tax-havens or to managing businesses
overseas.'** (Speech, Finance Houses Association, 25.1.79)

In the new Government's first budget in June 1979, the top
rates of tax were cut by 23p in the pound – from 83p to 60p.
Those on the higher rates found themselves very much
better off. Someone earning £50,000 a year had £4,000
more in their pocket.

**'Nations depend for their health, economically culturally
and psychologically, upon the achievements of a comparatively small number of talented and determined people, as
well as on the support of a skilled and devoted majority. It
was not possible for many of these talented people to believe
that we valued them, and what they could do for our nation,
when we maintained penal tax rates, decade after decade, in
order to please those who seemed to be motivated mainly by
envy.'** (Speech, Conservative Political Centre, 6.7.79)

To assuage any envy, Margaret Thatcher has assured the
country that little revenue comes in from high earners:

DID YOU KNOW? 🐖 **'A country's top rate of tax is a symbol. Very little revenue is
collected from people in this country who pay tax at the**

highest rates. **A top rate of 83% is not much of a revenue raiser, it is the symbol of British socialism – the symbol of envy.'** (Speech, Putney, 17.2.78)

'Very little revenue'? The cut in the top rate of tax saves the rich £662 million every year.

According to Treasury figures, 30% of income tax reliefs went to the richest 5% of the population. Which, as Mrs Thatcher was quick to point out,

'leaves 70% to go to the rest.' (*Hansard* 12.7.79)

The pattern of tax decisions has continued; the rich have got richer, and the poor poorer.

There are three types of wealth tax. Capital Gains Tax – paid by about 200,000 people – has been cut four times in the last four years.

Capital Transfer Tax is paid by approximately 150,000 people. They are £150 million a year better off after cuts in this tax.

Investment Income Surcharge was an additional tax paid by people with more than £70,000 invested. The tax was scrapped in 1984. The loss of revenue was £360 million – almost double what the Government cut from housing benefit to the poorest families in November 1983.

'Unnecessarily high rates of tax work not only to the economic disadvantage of Britain; they strike at the very roots of the free society in which Conservatives believe.' (*The Times* 21.2.76)

'What is opportunity if your only opportunity is to be equal?' (Eastbourne, 14.2.81)

Up, Up and Away – Prices

'The Ancient Romans, I believe, thought there was another criterion which should apply to those who could be entrusted with looking after their financial affairs. That was the criterion of being female. Yes, they set their mint in the temple not of a god but of a goddess.' (Lord Mayor's Banquet, 16.11.81)

'The success of the Government in getting down inflation and in holding it down is quite outstanding. When we were returned to power a 5% rate of inflation was thought impossible. We now regard 5% as high and we must get it down further.' (*Hansard*, 17.1.84)

In May 1979, when Margaret Thatcher became Prime Minister, inflation stood at 10.3%. By 1984 it was around 6%. But this is not the whole story.

'It has taken us a long time to realise that unless we elevate the reduction of inflation to a first priority the very fabric of society will fall apart.' (Speech, Chicago, 29.9.75)

After one year of her reign, her Government's policies had pushed inflation up to 21.9%.

'Inflation is the biggest destroyer of all – of industry, of jobs, of savings, of society. It is folly to diagnose the disease and know the cure but to lack the courage to prescribe or the tenacity to take the medicine. It is neither moral nor responsible for a government to spend beyond the nation's means – even for services which may be desirable.' (Speech, Conference of Conservative Trade Unionists, 1.11.80)

In November 1980, when she made this speech, inflation was 15.5% – half as much again as when she took office.

'It is an insidious evil. It has a morally debilitating influence on all aspects of our national life. It reduces the value of savings, it undermines financial agreements, it stimulates hostility between workers and employers over matters of pay. It encourages debt and it diminishes the prospects of jobs. It is a moral issue, not just an economic one.' (Speech from the pulpit of St Lawrence Jewry, 4.3.81)

'When inflation runs riot it is not simply cash that is carried away in suitcases, it is trust and honesty as well.' (Lord Mayor's Banquet, 15.11.82)

The pound in May 1979 was only worth 61p in April 1984. Inflation may be down, but prices have risen dramatically in the last five years. In her 1979 campaign Margaret Thatcher held high a bag of groceries that could be bought with £1 and compared it to a bag bought in 1974. In 1984 £1 will buy a loaf of bread and ½lb (250g) of butter.

In Opposition Margaret Thatcher once said:

'What prices have risen most? The answer was given in the House of Commons a few days ago. Note that the biggest increase came from industries that are under government control – coal, electricity and gas. Nationalised industries have a monopoly. If you want what they sell you have to pay what they charge.' (*News of the World*, 5.5.68)

Since 1979 it has been Margaret Thatcher's policy that gas and electricity prices should go up more than other prices. Gas went up by the rate of inflation plus 10% for three years: in 1980 by 27%; in 1981 by 25%; in 1982 by 22%. Electricity prices went up almost as much. In 1982–3 the Electricity Board made a profit of £332 million.

While on the subject of fuel, Britain has vast resources of oil. The profits and the oil tax revenues to the government are enormous: £500 million in 1978–9, and up to £8,900 million in 1983–4. How is this money to be used?

'We reject the socialist view that these [oil revenues] should be retained by the Government and used to increase state power by state intervention in industry. Instead we believe that this provides us with a means of reducing still further the necessary evil of personal taxation, so that once again it pays to work, to acquire skill and to take a risk.' (Speech, Glasgow, 9.1.78)

How has it been used?

'We are making provision for the future because a lot of that money is being invested overseas.' (BBC Television, 9.4.84)

Pennies From Heaven – Welfare and Benefits

'No one wishes to make cuts in public expenditure, but we are up against the reality that no government can urge a nation to live beyond its means.' (*Hansard*, 27.11.79)

'You cannot look after the hard-up people in society unless you are accruing enough wealth to do so. Good intentions are not enough. You do need hard cash.' (BBC Television, 11.7.77)

However:

'Economic realities and administrative difficulties are the two great modifiers of policies, but they are too readily used as an excuse. The reason why a particular policy has been delayed may be given as "no money", but it's more likely that the government has preferred to spend money elsewhere.' (*Daily Telegraph*, 17.3.79)

Mrs Thatcher's Government has chosen to increase spending on defence and law and order and to cut spending on housing, education and welfare provision. Their policies also led to the soaring increase in unemployment. As a result the rise in the social security budget and the tax revenue lost as people lose jobs have thwarted their attempts to cut public spending.

'A government may provide a framework of social services, a safety–net through which none may fall. But the many deeds of mercy, the myriad of acts of human kindness which give life its dignity and meaning, these are the work of individuals.' (Speech, Institution of Electrical Engineers, 27.6.82)

37

'Our task will be so much easier when we have reduced public spending.' (Lord Mayor's Banquet, 12.11.79)

But in 1984, Nigel Lawson, Chancellor of the Exchequer, said:

'We do not need to cut our spending overall but we do need to stick to our published plans.' (Speech, Scottish Conservative Party, 9.5.84).

The Government's plans for 1983–4 were published in 1980. Public borrowing – the cash a government has to borrow to supplement tax revenues – was to be £2,500 million. In March 1983, estimates showed that it would actually be £8,000 million. When the final figures were calculated in 1984, public borrowing was expected to be £10,000 million.

In an attempt to keep to its plans, the Government has had to prune spending where it can.

PROMISES, PROMISES ☛ 'I am not saying, of course, that the State has no welfare functions. This would be wholly against the tradition of my party. We have always believed there must be a level of well-being below which a citizen must not be a allowed to fall.' (Speech from the pulpit of St Lawrence Jewry, 30.3.78)

In 1980 unemployment benefit was cut:

'I believe it was right to cut the increase in unemployment benefits by some 5% because it is right to have a large difference between those in work and those out of work.' (*The Times*, 2.5.80)

In 1982 the benefit was taxed:

'Most people would think it right that those who are in work should be better off than those who unfortunately cannot find work.' (*Hansard*, 18.12.82)

Pensioners have suffered too. Before the election in 1979 Margaret Thatcher had said:

'We pledge to maintain the value of retirement pensions in terms of what they will buy in the shops.' (Speech, Gravesend, 17.4.79)

What she meant was that the Government would change the method of calculating pension increases. Before, these had been linked to prices or wages, whichever rose faster; in future, pensions would only rise in line with the Retail Price Index. Therefore, they would keep up with the cost of living, but never get better.

'It would be misleading to suggest that the restraints on public expenditure the Government have been forced to introduce could be achieved without any consequences at all for the elderly.' (*Hansard*, 22.11.79)

In November 1980 the pensioners' increase was delayed for two weeks – saving the Government £60 million.

In November 1981 the pensioners' increase was 2% lower than the rate of inflation – pensioners would be able to afford less in the shops. No wonder Margaret Thatcher had once said people should

'save towards a pension in their old age instead of depending on the state pension.' (*Building Societies Gazette*, 10.67)

Pensioners also suffered with the introduction of housing

'Iron entered my soul. You need a touch of steel. Otherwise you become like India rubber.' (BBC Radio 4, 30.3.80)

'We should not expect the State to appear in the guise of an extravagant good fairy at every christening, a loquacious companion at every stage of life's journey, the unkown mourner at every funeral.' (Airey Neave Memorial Lecture, 3.3.80)

benefit. In the switch from rent and rate rebates to this new benefit, it was estimated that 2.5 million claimants lost out. And when cuts in the benefit were announced in November 1983, another 2.2 million families lost out – over half of them pensioners.

Even Tory MPs objected: *'Those who will suffer will be the pensioners with savings, a small occupational pension or part-time earnings, low-income families caught in the poverty trap, and those who have taken the opportunity to buy their council house.'* (Andrew Bowden MP, *Guardian*, 13.2.84)

DID YOU KNOW? ☛ **'It is neither moral nor responsible for a government to spend beyond the nation's means – even for services which may be desirable.'** (Conference of Conservative Trade Unionists, 1.11.80)

The disabled have also suffered. Mrs Thatcher says:

'The International Year of Disabled People will, I hope, call forth a lot more voluntary effort on behalf of the disabled. Most of us think it is more laudable to do something for oneself than to get up and take a public stance on an issue to try to persuade the government to do it.' (*Hansard*, 13.1.81)

When Jack Ashley MP suggested a review of benefits to the disabled, Mrs Thatcher replied:

'There is little point and perhaps some danger in developing plans for a new benefit for disabled people when we do not know what the country can afford and when.' (*Hansard*, 13.1.81)

She justifies her stand-on-your-own-two-feet policy:

'Our public expenditure has been prudent and realistic.' (*Hansard*, 28.10.81)

'This enthusiasm for voluntary help is not the result of the need to reduce government spending. There are those who carp and imply that the volunteer is just a cheaper substitute for salaried staff; quite the contrary. The voluntary movement is at the heart of our social welfare provision.' (Speech to the WRVS, 19.1.81)

'We all recognise that the individual can only achieve his full dignity and make the best use of his talents in a society based on freedom under the law – a law which is fearlessly and impartially administered. (Foundation meeting of the European Democratic Union, 24.4.78)

That law can be changed very fast when it might cost the Government money. A ruling that the sick and disabled could claim a one-off payment from social security for medical aids (like false limbs) was reached on 3 November 1983. On 5 November, the Social Security Minister Rhodes Boyson tabled new legislation – the next day disabled and sick claimants had lost the right to finance for medical aids.

'The relentless growth of the public sector has put a crushing burden on the private wealth-creating sector. We must therefore contain the cost of the public sector.' (Lord Mayor's Banquet, 10.11.80)

And:

'The more people are able to produce, the more we shall be able to spend on desirable social services.' (*Hansard*, 25.10.79)

Margaret Thatcher's economic policies have led to the sharpest drop in output since the 1920s. Manufacturing output has declined by 20% since she took office. In 1983 – for the first time since the Industrial Revolution – Britain imported more than it exported.

In 1971, Rhodes Boyson wrote: '*The state spends all its energies taking money from the energetic, sucessful and thrifty to give to the idle, the failures and the feckless*' (*Down With the Poor*, Churchill Press, 1971).

In a review of benefits paid to the 'idle' – the unemployed – the Government estimated that in 1979 £108 million was lost through welfare fraud.

The loss to the Government through tax evasion (a crime committed largely by the wealthy) is between £3,000 million and £3,500 million a year. This figure does not include VAT evasion.

'I promise you this – I won't make empty promises.'
(Party Political Broadcast, 2.4.79)

To ensure that those who are labelled 'scroungers' and 'fiddlers' were brought to book, 1,050 extra officers were employed by the DHSS in 1980.

To crack down on those who 'get away with' not paying their taxes, the Inland Revenue appointed 70 new staff in 1981.

In 1984, Rhodes Boyson's department was planning to stop all home visits to help claimants complete their forms, and switch the 2,000 people employed on this work to investigating fraud.

'I came to office with one deliberate intent: to change Britain from a dependent to a self-reliant society; from a give-it-to-me to a do-it-yourself nation; a get-up-and-go instead of a sit-back-and-wait-for-it Britain.' (Speech, Small Businesses Bureau, 8.2.84)

Home Sweet Home – Housing

'We stand for personal and independent ownership against state ownership. Through measures to encourage home ownership, Conservative governments have helped to spread wealth on a wide scale to people who, like most of us, started with nothing.' (Speech, Young Conservatives National Conference, 12.2.78)

'Above all, never throw in the towel when you are within an ace of success.' (Speech, Conservative Party Conference, 17.10.81)

When Margaret Roberts married Denis Thatcher in 1951, she moved into his smart London flat in Swan Court, Chelsea. With the arrival of the twins, Mark and Carol, it felt a little cramped, so they rented the adjoining flat, and knocked the two into one.

But the countryside called and they moved to a house called The Dormers, in Locks Bottom, Farnborough, Kent. Margaret Thatcher described it as:

'A medium-sized house with five bedrooms standing in one and a half acres of garden. We have an excellent daily help who keeps the house in spotless order. Nannie looks after the children's rooms and their clothes.'(*Evening News*, London, 25.2.60)

'There is no safe corner where the inefficient can shelter.' (*Hansard*, 12.11.81)

They had, after all, done exactly what she believed all young couples should do:

HEART OF THE MATTER ☛

'It is important that young couples purchase their own home as early as possible. The chances are that they will never then come to be dependent on the state.' (*Daily Telegraph*, 26.4.69)

Margaret, Denis and the children had now moved into a larger house, in three acres of garden, with a tennis court and a swimming pool.

'As for being out of touch with ordinary people that's just utter nonsense. The people who say that just don't know what kind of life I lead. People know I have a sizeable house in the country and they confuse size with wealth. I don't mind telling you that the house I wanted was several thousand pounds more than the one we got. In fact we're trying to sell it at the moment because I find it very difficult to run two homes.' (*Sunday Express*, 16.1.77)

The house was duly sold and they bought another, close to Parliament, in Flood Street, Chelsea. Then they rented a flat in Scotney Castle, Lamberhurst, a National Trust property; they still had the problem of running two homes. But owning your own home means more than just a roof over your head:

'Provision of houses is the most urgent social service of all. It will be the duty of a Conservative government to spare no effort to increase the number of houses built per year. After the needs of defence have been met, we shall give the housing priority over all other forms of building.' (Margaret Roberts' election leaflet, 1951)

'Freedom is not just a passive ideal reserved for political speeches. It means freedom to act, to do things for yourself and your family, to benefit from personal endeavour, to own property . . . That is why we Conservatives put forward positive plans for owning your own home, whether it be built privately or by the council. That way you have a real stake in Britain.' (*Daily Telegraph*, 9.10.74)

Shelter, the housing charity, estimates that there is a housing shortage of over 800,000 homes. In 1983, council house building was down to an all-time low.

'Under this Government the property-owning democracy is growing fast. And the basic foundation is the family home.' (Manifesto, 1983)

In 1979 there were 10,000 people in arrears with mortgages; in 1984 there were 32,000.

There are one and a quarter million people on council waiting lists. Shelter estimates that there are 80,000 families accepted as homeless by local authorities. Many are turned away – not sufficiently homeless to warrant being housed. Many are put into bed-and-breakfast accommodation, at a cost of up to £70 million a year.

'Our goal is to make Britain the best housed nation in Europe.' (Manifesto, 1983)

But:

* Over one million dwellings are unfit for habitation.
* One million lack basic amenities.
* Four million need repairs of more than £2,500 each.
* Nearly 600,000 households are overcrowded, with more than one person per room.
* The homes of owner-occupiers are now five times more likely to need repairs than council homes.

The Government has worked hard to extend the freedom of home ownership:

'Mothers with small children living in tower blocks will, under a Conservative government, now have three options: to carry on renting, to put down an option to purchase the flat within a reasonable time or to purchase the flat. That seems to me to enlarge the freedom and possibilities available to such people.' (*Hansard*, 24.5.79)

'If you have conviction people are much more likely to come out and support you. Most of the great faiths upon which our own moral values are founded would never have got started if their prophets had gone out to the people and said: "Brothers, I believe in consensus".' (*News of the World*, 20.9.81)

'One thing aggravates me more than anything else – inefficiency. I can be very sharp about that.' (*Daily Express*, 7.3.62)

Before Margaret Thatcher's government insisted on selling three-quarters of a million council houses, the 'possibilities available' might have included a transfer to a house with a garden. Only 2% of council property sales have been flats; only the best properties are sold.

'We would surely wish to look forward in the long run to a nation in which only a small minority of the people live as municipal tenants.' (Speech, Bow Group, 6.5.78)

Two-thirds of people on supplementary benefits are council tenants, and are therefore unable to buy property.

The sale of council houses is only one part of a policy designed to reduce the amount spent on council housing:

'The Government's medium-term strategy of reducing public spending relies principally on the achievement of the planned reduction in housing expenditure.' (Commons Environment Committee, HMSO, 1979–80)

Between 1980 and 1984, government spending on housing was cut by over a third. The share of public spending that goes on housing has dwindled from 7½% in 1978–9 to a projected 2% in 1985–6. At the same time, council rents have risen by 130%.

A council tenant wrote to Mrs Thatcher about the poor condition of her flat. Matthew Parris MP wrote:

'At Mrs Thatcher's request I am replying. I hope you will not think me too blunt if I say that it may well be that your council accommodation is unsatisfactory but considering the fact that you have been unable to buy your own accommodation you are lucky to have been given something which the rest of us are paying for out of our taxes.'(6.3.79)

In 1981–2 the subsidy to council tenants was £183 per person. The tax subsidy to people with mortgages was £285 per person. In 1983–4 the Treasury handed out £3,000 million in tax relief to people with mortgages. In the same year the total housing budget was £2,700 million.

In May 1984, the Government announced new plans to encourage the sale of yet more council property. Making the announcement, Margaret Thatcher said:

'I want everyone to be a man of property; that's the way we'll get one nation.' (BBC Radio 4, 6.5.84)

Could Try Harder –
Education

'I think comprehensive schools will have gone out in 10 or 15 years time.' (*Daily Express*, 16.3.70)

'We want to give the best educational opportunity to every pupil.' (*Hansard*, 31.10.69)

Margaret Thatcher had just taken up her post as Opposition spokeswoman for Education. In 1970 she became Secretary of State for Education. During her period in office she made bold claims about expansion and improvement in the education system:

'I have nailed my flag to the primary school mast; that must have top priority.' (Speech, Association of Education Committees, 28.10.70)

'I want to see continued progress, with reduction of class size in primary schools and the improving of their staffing ratios.' (Ibid.)

In 1984 there were one million children in primary schools in classes with over 30 children, and 130,000 in classes with over 35.

'I believe that pupil/teacher ratios provide a better index of staffing standards than class size.' (*Hansard*, 19.11.70)

Ratios confuse and conceal the truth. Between 1980 and

1983 pupil/teacher ratios fell from 18.7 pupils per teacher to 18.1 pupils per teacher. But in 1983, school inspectors found primary schools with ratios as high as 31 pupils per teacher.

Between 1979 and 1983, the total number of children at school in England fell by over 800,000. Had the Government not decided to cut education expenditure, the pupil/teacher ratio could have been as low as 17 to one.

In 1970, when Mrs Thatcher, then Secretary of State for Education, stopped the provision of free milk to primary schools, she became known as the 'Milk Snatcher'.

'I think we might have put it [milk] on sale. From free school milk to no milk was a big jump – too big a jump.' (*Daily Mail*, 25.8.73)

'I realised there was going to be a label tied to me because of the milk, but I've gone on steadily doing the job and I must confess the record really is pretty impressive.' (*Liverpool Daily Post*, 21.2.72)

Under the 1980 Education Act schools no longer have to provide milk – or meals – except to children of families living on benefits.

'I am making no promises now, but my hope is that over a period of five years we shall be in sight of the elimination of the primary schools built in the nineteenth century.' (Press conference, 28.10.70)

In 1984, nearly half of the schools in Inner London were built before 1900.

'School buildings do matter. Usually in new schools one finds pupils take tremendous care of the school, its buildings and surroundings, and that in itself is an education.' (Speech, National Union of Teachers Conference, 3.4.72)

In 1984, Her Majesty's Inspectorate reported: *'Problems in secondary schools include overcrowding, poor maintenance, drab appearance. Almost all primary schools are short of books . . . there is a particular shortage of both text and library books in many of the secondary schools.'*

Because of growing unemployment, the number of 16-year-olds now staying on at school has risen from 19%, in 1979, to 22% in 1983–4. In Opposition, Mrs Thatcher said:

'I believe the polytechnics have an enormous potential; but they will never achieve what we want them to on the basis of the present Government's spending plans on education. Education spending should rise faster than the average.' (*Guardian*, 17.2.70)

Since 1980, the Government has imposed a limit on the funding for further education. In 1983–4, all but eight out of 29 polytechnics were expected to take in more students, while their funding was cut. One example is Birmingham polytechnic, which had its funding cut by 6%, but had to take in 9% more students.

PROMISES, PROMISES ☛ **'Our main concern is to see that there is provision for the varying abilities and requirements of children and the doors of opportuniy are kept open to all children to go on, if they are capable, to 'O'- and 'A'-levels and to University.'** (*Hansard*, 31.10.69)

Between 1981 and 1983, university places were cut by 5,000, to a total of 69,000. There were more than 157,000 applicants for these places.

'There are in fact more of our age group coming through with graduate degrees than there are in most other countries.

That's the acid test: not how many go in, but how many come out with degrees.' (BBC Radio 4, 30.3.83)

'I believe that uniformity is death to a virile system of education and we should not say one system and none other.' (*Hansard*, 17.4.70)

In 1980, despite cuts in education spending, the Government announced the Assisted Places Scheme, to subsidise more children going to public and independent schools. The scheme cost £22.5 million in 1984.

'The overall picture is one of gradual deterioration with a few bright but many black spots.' (*Education Observed*, Department of Education, 1984)

But let us remember:

'It is still the law of the land that there should be an act of worship and of assembly at the beginning of every school day. Anybody who tries to deprive children of the pleasure of singing hymns may deprive them of an experience they may otherwise never have.' (*Hansard*, 10.11.83)

All Stitched Up – Health

'At this time I feel one should recall the words of the first Queen Elizabeth. "It would involve temporary discomfort, not only to them that being sick received the medicine and in the taste felt some bitterness, but yet recover health and strength to save their lives …" The second Queen Elizabeth's first minister cannot put it much better.' (Speech, Conservative Trades Unionists' Conference, 1.11.80)

'The National Health Service is safe with us.' (Conservative Party Conference, 8.10.82)

'We at Guy's and other hospitals in London are refusing emergency babies. Some of them are dying. I have evidence of that,' said Dr Michael Joseph, a consultant paediatrician. 'There is a national shortage of intensive care cots throughout the country. I am very surprised that any government does not consider babies to be a priority' (Daily Telegraph, 4.10.83). Guy's had recently closed a children's ward because it could not afford to keep it open on its existing budget.

In 1979 there were 532,000 people on NHS waiting lists. In 1983 there were 640,000.

'There is of course no waiting list for the treatment of renal [kidney] failure; untreated patients die not long after their condition is diagnosed.' (Report of the Chief Medical Officer, DHSS, 1982)

Each year 1,000 people suffering from kidney failure go untreated through lack of funds.

GOOD NEWS ☞ 'I want to make it absolutely clear that the Conservative Party has no plans for new health charges.' (Daily Mirror, 14.11.79)

52

In May 1979, prescription charges were 20p. In June 1979 they went up to 45p. In April 1980 they went up again – to 70p.

'**The principle that adequate health care should be provided for all, regardless of ability to pay, must be the foundation of any arrangements for funding the health service.**' (*Hansard*, 1.12.81)

In 1982 charges rose to £1.30.

'**From time to time prescription charges have to be raised.**' (*Hansard*, 8.3.83)

That April they went up to £1.40. A year later they climbed again – to £1.60.

Dental charges have risen from a maximum of £30 in 1979 to £95 in 1983.

'*It is not our intention to reduce spending on the National Health Service.*' (Manifesto, 1979)

Spending has indeed gone up, from £7 billion in 1979 to £14.7 billion in 1983, but the rise in spending has not been sufficient to meet the growing needs of the NHS. There are more and more old people in the population, and medical technology is increasingly expensive. The NHS needs a budget increase of 1.5% a year just to maintain present standards. The government is providing only 0.5%. That means a real cut in resources. According to a *Guardian* survey, 109 hospitals were closed between 1979 and 1983. Of the 192 health authorities in England and Wales, 21 said they had closed hospitals, wards or clinics. Administrators were '*universally critical*' and nearly all of them were '*vitriolic and some apoplectic*' (*Guardian*, 18.1.84).

'**It's like a nurse looking after a sick patient. Which is the better nurse? The one who smothers the patient with sympathy and says, "Never mind dear; there, there, you just lie back and I'll bring you all your meals." Or the nurse who says, "Now come on, shake your self out of it. I know you've had an operation yesterday. It's time you took a few steps. That's right dear, that's right. Now get back and take a few more tomorrow." Which is the one most likely to get the results? The one who says "Come on, you can do it." That's me.**' (Independent Radio News, 30.11.80)

'I feel there are times when we have lost our vision of the future, and we know that where there is no vision, the people must surely perish.' (*The Times*, 21.2.75)

'We are proud of the way we have shielded the National Health Service from the recession.' (Manifesto, 1983)

Since 1979, 10,865 hospital beds have been cut.

Three months into their first term of office, the Conservatives announced there would be a 'squeeze' of £100 million on NHS spending. '*We know the squeeze will hurt,*' said Patrick Jenkin, Social Services Secretary. '*Naturally,*' he added, '*some health authorities are faced with the need to make real cuts this year...*' (Labour Research, 2.80).

A DHSS report on NHS property announced that £2,000 million was needed just to bring existing hospital buildings to a minimum acceptable standard.

'I should point out that the number of doctors in the National Health Service has increased by 2,000, and nurses by 10,000.' (*Hansard*, 16.2.81)

The Halsbury Report of 1974 recommended that medical staff should work shorter hours. The change was eventually implemented in 1980–81. The Royal College of Nursing estimated that, as a result, 16,000 more staff were needed – 10,000 of those trained nurses – simply to maintain the service. '*The total number of unemployed doctors is now 2,000–3,000 and rising*' (British Medical Association, 2.84).

In 1981, the last year for which unemployment figures were collected according to profession, there were 10,971 nurses out of work.

In August 1982, Mrs Thatcher had her varicose veins removed at the £115-a-day privately-owned BUPA Fitzroy Nuffield Hospital in London. Private hospital treatment for varicose veins costs between £400 and £700. There are about one million varicose veins sufferers in this country in need of treatment.

'I pay my full whack to the National Health Service and I make no demands on it.' (*Hansard*, 7.11.83)

➤ DID YOU KNOW?

In 1983 Mrs Thatcher had an eye operation at the private Christian Hospital in Windsor. It later emerged that the operation required equipment to be borrowed from the nearby King Edward VII NHS hospital.

'The NHS is a marvel.' (*Daily Telegraph*, 23.12.83)

The Conservative government has done a great deal to undermine the NHS by promoting private medicine.
* Tax relief has been given to many who subscribe to private health schemes.
* Restrictions on the building of private hospitals have been lifted.
* The Health Services Board was abolished in 1982 – as a result, the number of private beds in NHS hospitals has increased.
* Consultants' contracts have been revised so that they can take on more private work without loss of salary from the NHS.
* Health Authorities have been forced to use services carried out by private contractors.

The Greenfield Report of February 1982 showed that if the NHS stopped using brand–name drugs, £170 million could be saved. The Report's recommendations were ignored. In contrast, a saving of £40 million was made in 1983–4 when 5,000 health service jobs were cut.

'We believe that competition is the best and only final test of efficiency.' (*Daily Telegraph*, 7.3.79)

In September 1983, Norman Fowler, Secretary of State for Social Services, issued a circular telling all District Health Authorities to consider privatising catering, cleaning and laundry services. His rationale: *'The government believes that the use of private contractors under carefully drawn and properly controlled contracts can provide the most cost-effective measures.'*

55

One guided missile destroyer cost £85 million in 1980; £76 million could have paid for three 1,000–bed hospitals.

Linda Lockyer, regional principal at the DHSS, said in a letter which was leaked in April 1984: *'None of these factors – such as conditions of service, including protection of present conditions and rights – feature in our policy advice which is firmly that the lowest tenderer should be appointed.'*

Documents leaked to the *Guardian* in March 1984 revealed that Kenneth Clarke and his junior, John Patten, knew that NHS staff in Cornwall could run the hospital laundry for £47,320 less than a private firm – the private firm won the contract. (This firm, Kneels, is a subsidiary of the Johnson Group which donated £1,535 to the Conservative Party between 1980 and 1982.) The bill for redundancies came to £24,000 – 40 jobs were lost.

'I congratulate the many local authorities that are trying to use private contractors, whose costs are usually lower, as much as possible. Of course employing private contractors on a contractual basis ... means that local authorities do not have to provide inflation-proof pensions.' (*Hansard*, 12.1.81)

'In the community we must do more to help people help themselves, and families to look after their own. We must also encourage the voluntary movement and self-help groups working in partnership with the statutory services.' (Manifesto, 1979)

The Black Report on inequalities in health (DHSS, 1980) found that babies born to skilled or unskilled workers run a 33% greater risk of infant mortality than those born to middle-class families.

Margaret Thatcher wants to reduce state support for the old and the sick by encouraging voluntary organisations which provide:

'stimulus to the partnership between the public sector and individual generosity.' (*Hansard*, 12.1.81)

As services are 'squeezed', voluntary organisations and individuals have to fill the gaps. 'Individual generosity' is not always rewarded, however. Married women who stay at home to look after their relatives are not eligible for Invalid Care Allowance. (In 1982 the DHSS estimated that 80,000 married women would be eligible if the Invalid Care Allowance were extended.)

'The treatment of the elderly, the mentally handicapped and the mentally ill will continue to command our particular attention.' (Manifesto, 1983)

The number of elderly people is projected to rise by 13% by 1993. Cuts in geriatric services and the loss of hospital beds needed by old people has caused consultants to speak out:

Deaf people wanting hearing–aids now face waiting–lists of up to two and a half years.

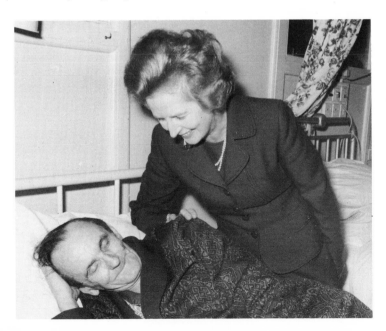

Defence research and development cost £1,497 million in 1980; £40 million was spent on medical research.

'*We are finding more and more that we are having to press reluctant relatives to take back patients. I hate having to do it but we have no choice,*' said Dr Audrey Ahmet, consultant at Ealing Hospital, London (*Sunday Times*, 24.7.83).

The Government is committed to closing down many large mental hospitals in favour of 'community care'. Dr Patrick Campbell, a consultant at Friern Barnet mental hospital in London, which has already suffered cuts, said: '*My fear is that many of those discharged have disappeared on to the streets, or live in appalling squalor because of community neglect.*' Dr Malcolm Weller, another consultant at the hospital, said: '*At current rates of developing community care, it will take 40 years to provide for the people who have already been discharged, never mind those who are supposed to go over in the next ten years.*' An advisor to the National Schizophrenic Society, Dr Pamela Jenkinson,

concludes: '*The Government sees this as a perfect opportunity to save money. They are using the goodwill over community care to implement cuts*' (*The Times*, 28.3.84).

In March 1982, the Social Services Committee reported to the DHSS that there would be a 9% cut in hospital and community care during 1982–3.

'The Government have made clear the high esteem in which they hold the nurses.' (*Hansard*, 17.12.81)

'I do not believe that nurses would do anything so detrimental to the interests of their patients as go on strike.' (*Hansard*, 8.7.82)

But the nurses did go on strike that year. Despite the settlement *after* the dispute, nurses' pay is 23% less than that of the average non-manual worker. While an 18-year-old police constable earned £6,708 per annum in 1983, a student nurse earned £3,695.

In June 1983, 95% of ancillary health staff were still on a basic wage of £77 per week, some of the lowest paid workers in Britain.

The Royal College of Nursing said: '*Nurses want the public to know that standards of care are already threatened, that staffing on wards hovers just above danger level and that out in the community increased numbers of patients are over-burdening community care and making good nursing practices practically impossible*' (*Guardian*, 29.9.83).

Mrs Thatcher says:

'This government has an excellent record over the National Health Service.' (*Hansard*, 13.3.84)

◥VITAL STATISTIC

The Big Match – Unions

'There are people in this country who are great destroyers; they wish to destroy the kind of free society we have ... Many of these people are in unions.' (Thames Television, 24.4.79)

'Millions of British workers go in fear of union power.' (Conservative Party Conference, 13.10.79)

So long as the unions agree with Mrs Thatcher's policies, all will be well:

'There is no problem about my getting on with trade unions or trade unions getting on with me, provided we both are interested in getting a flourishing Britain.' (BBC Television, 23.2.76)

But they must remember their place:

'I respect the trade unions for looking after their people at work. But I expect them to respect that politics must lie with the politicians. The role of the trade unions is not a political role.' (BBC Television, 17.7.78)

'I hate class. It seems to stem from the early days of class, clash, conflict. People no longer think that way.' (*Daily Express*, 27.1.77)

But conflict was clearly in the minds of Tory Party leaders: *'The eventual battle should be on the ground chosen by us, in a field we think can be won (railways, British Leyland, the civil service, or steel),'* wrote Nicholas Ridley MP, in a document leaked to the *Economist* magazine in May 1978. It was the final report of a Tory Party policy group on the nationalised industries. The battle with the unions would be over the methods used to make those industries profitable: this *'might mean that men would be laid off or uneconomic plants would be closed down, or whole businesses sold off or liquidated.'*

In the autumn of 1979, closures in the steel industry were announced and a 2% pay offer made to the steel workers. A strike was called.

'I do not believe that people who go on strike in this country have a legitimate cause.' (*Hansard*, 17.6.82)

During the firemen's prolonged dispute with the previous Labour Government, Mrs Thatcher said:

'We must recognise that the firemen are in a different position from other people. We rely on them and I am prepared to pay them a bit more.' (Radio interview 21.11.77)

In the following year, Matthew Parris MP wrote on her behalf to a fireman in the Midlands: *'The Conservative Party will support any reasonable offer of pay or conditions within the fire service which has been made previous to its return to power.'*

But in November 1980, with the Tories back in office, the firemen were told they were getting only 6% instead of the 18.8% agreed under the previous deal.

Civil servants, another group identified by Nicholas Ridley as easily defeatable, were provoked into a dispute in early 1981. It lasted for 21 weeks. The unions estimated

'I always appreciate the other person's problem.' (*Daily Express*, 13.3.80)

that £8,000 million was lost in revenue and £140 million incurred in interest charges on extra borrowing.

The health workers met the same stubbornness in 1982. The train drivers were also defeated that year. The Post Office engineers were beaten in 1983. The Government had taken on the unions in the public sector one by one.

'In the private sector there are excellent industrial relations on the whole between management and shop floor. It's not "we" and "they", it's "all of us". And they're doing some superb work. If you look at some of the trade union difficulties we're having now, you'll find they're pretty nearly all in the public sector. The public sector, where it has the monopoly, it has the muscle.' (Thames Television, 18.2.82)

One person brought in to help deal with the muscle of the public sector unions was Ian MacGregor. He moved as deputy chairman of British Leyland to chairman of the British Steel Corporation in 1980 (and became chairman of the National Coal Board in 1983). Mrs Thatcher said:

'He has taken businesses, has built them up, created employment, and expanded them.' (BBC Radio 4, 4.5.80)

While he was at British Steel the number of employees fell from 166,400 to 81,100.

But it was the miners who were most feared. They had brought down Ted Heath's government in 1974.

In 1981, Margaret Thatcher wasn't yet ready to take them on. In February, 50,000 miners walked out in protest after the announcement of pit closures. Within five days the £250 million required to keep the pits open had been found:

'It's no good dreaming about U-turns. There are none available.' (*Observer*, 3.8.80)

'We really want to put as much money into the future of coal as we possibly can.' (*Hansard*, 17.2.81)

By 1984 the Government was better prepared. Pit closures and the loss of 20,000 jobs were announced in March: the majority of miners came out on strike. Mrs Thatcher said:

'This strike is not of the Government's making.' (*Hansard*, 14.7.84)

The Ridley plan had spelt out the steps the Government should take:

'Build up maximum coal stocks, particularly at the power stations'.
* *'Make contingency plans for the import of coal'.*
* *'Encourage the recruitment of non-union lorry drivers by haulage companies to help remove coal where necessary'.*

Coal stocks had been built up from 14 million tonnes in 1979 to over 24 million tonnes by the end of 1983.

'[Stockpiling] is economic madness in any terms, bad for business enterprise and bad for the morale of those in the coal industry.' (*Hansard*, 5.12.67)

She was in Opposition then; now Mrs Thatcher was preparing for a long battle. She said:

'We are not going to intervene in the coal dispute.' (Speech, Scottish Conservative Conference, 11.5.84)

But documents leaked to the *Daily Mirror* show that the Government had intervened – by persuading British Rail to settle with its workers, then in dispute, in order to prevent

'When hecklers stand up ... I get a mental jump for joy. It gives me something to get my teeth into – and the audiences love it.' (*Daily Graphic*, 9.10.51)

63

prevent the two unions joining forces.

'In the Falklands we had to fight the enemy without. Here the enemy is within and it is much more difficult to fight, but just as dangerous to liberty.' (Speech, 1922 Committee, 19.7.84)

The dispute has cost the Government hundreds of millions of pounds. After five months of strikes, Nigel Lawson, Chancellor of the Exchequer, said that it was a *'worthwhile investment'*.

Ridley had also anticipated: *'There should be a large mobile squad of police equipped and prepared to uphold the law against violent picketing. Good, non-union drivers should be recruited to cross picket lines with police protection.'*

In the same week that miners from the Kent coalfields were refused access to the Midlands by British police, Margaret Thatcher condemned

'the ruthless suppression of the Polish people's efforts to secure some of those civil and political freedoms which we take for granted.' (*The Times*, 26.3.84)

And trade union membership had just been banned for civil servants working in the Government's Communications Headquarters at Cheltenham.

It is now almost impossible for a union to win an industrial dispute without breaking the law.

'[Limiting union power] was the theme running through our 1980 and 1982 Employment Acts by which we curbed the abuse of arbitrary power; in the closed shop, by providing shop-floor ballots; on the picket line, by making secondary picketing unlawful.'(*Hansard*, 22.6.83)

* It is now illegal to picket anywhere but your own place of work – you cannot picket the headquarters of your company or a place where your work has been transferred during a strike.
* Trade unions are now liable for damages as a result of strikes, for the first time since 1906. Enormous fines have already been imposed.
* Solidarity action (for example, striking in sympathy for another union) is illegal.
* To establish a closed shop, 80% of the workers must vote 'yes' in a secret ballot.
* Government funds are available for secret ballots.

The Employment Acts have been used. In 1983, the courts ruled that NGA pickets of Eddie Shah's printing plant in Warrington were illegal – even though their members work had been transferred there. The union was fined over half a million pounds.

'The employer has rightly sought the protection of the courts. The protection of the law is there for every citizen in the land and it has to be used.' (*Hansard*, 1.12.83)

Thatcher's law broke the strike. Yet, said Mrs Thatcher:

'The law is wholly separate from politics.' (*Hansard*, 1.12.83)

The Ridley document had also suggested stopping benefit to strikers' families: *'The greatest deterrent to any strike would be to cut off the money supply to the strikers and make the union finance them.'*
    This legislation was promised in the 1979 Manifesto.

'We're not very enamoured of it [the benefit cut] **at the**

'I do not think it is advisable to seek head on clashes on great issues.' (*Daily Mirror*, 8.10.75)

DID YOU KNOW?

65

moment. There would be some people drawn out on strike who are not members of trade unions and what do you do? Deem them to have strike pay which they couldn't possibly have?' London Weekend Television, 6.1.80)

Six weeks later, Mrs Thatcher had made up her mind:

'We stated in our Manifesto that we would deem certain amounts to be paid from union funds and to be set against supplementary benefits. I am happy to say those plans are going ahead.' (*Hansard*, 14.2.80)

Steel workers were on strike at this time.

'I am worried about the steelworkers' wives. They have been on restricted payments for ten weeks and that must be pretty tough.' (*Guardian*, 15.3.80)

On 26 March, the payments to strikers' families were cut by £12 a week (a cut subsequently increased to £15 a week). Strikers themselves get no benefit and many unions have no strike fund.

'I have a weapon as well as legislation. It's persuasion, it's reality, it is events and it is the combination of those which is making people look at all of their responsibilities differently.' (London Weekend Television, 6.1.80)

As unemployment has risen, days lost through strikes have fallen. Nine million days were lost in 1978, the last full year of Labour Government. In 1980, the figure was nearly twelve million. In 1981, it was down to 4.2 million.

'The number of strikes is the lowest in 40 years – not bad for a Conservative government.' (*Time*, 2.81)

By 1983, 3.6 million days were lost through strikes. Douglas Wass, Permanent Secretary of the Treasury, said: '*What has happened in shopfloor behaviour through fear and anxiety is much greater than I think could have been achieved by more co-operative methods. That is a surprise to me.*' (The Times, 31.3.83)

'There are people exercising power and leading political factions who seem to be moved by narrow, brutal and irrational impulses. Their view of their own self-interest is so blinkered as to leave no space for purely human values, for peaceful negotiations or for economic advancement.' (Lord Mayor's Banquet, 10.11.80)

On the Beat – Law and Order

'Let us make this country safe to walk in.' (Party Political Broadcast, 30.4.79)

'The most disturbing threat to freedom and security is the growing disrespect for the rule of law. Yet respect for the rule of law is the basis of a free and civilised life. We will restore it, re-establishing the supremacy of Parliament and giving it the right priority against crime.' (Manifesto, 1979)

What are the causes of crime?

'If you have been led to believe that personal property is wicked and that ownership is contrary to pure socialist morality then naturally you will be disposed to denigrate the values which are associated with personal property. You will despise independence, thrift, self-denial and you will be less shocked by violence and disorder. We'll sweep the country clean of Socialism.' (*Daily Telegraph*, 22.2.75)

Or more simply:

DID YOU KNOW? ☞ 'I regard all those ... who want to destroy our way of life as Left. They are the people who want to disregard the ballot box. Disregard the rule of law. Your communism is ... the left foot of socialism and your fascism is the right foot of it

'... the fascist left and the communist left ... The problem of hooligans and the terrible problem of the marches ... if you can't get at it by self-discipline you have to get at it by deterrence.' (*Daily Telegraph*, 5.5.76)

What about unemployment? In 1982, when Michael Foot asked the Prime Minister about the relationship between crime and unemployment, Mrs Thatcher said:

'No, sir, there is not a direct relationship in any way ...' (*Hansard*, 16.3.82)

Some of her team admit the connection. Leaked documents from the Central Policy Review Staff (better known as the Think Tank) said: *'From the point of view of law and order, the fact that unemployment leaves some potentially troublesome youngsters with nothing to do is justifiable cause for anxiety. By the end of 1983, between 50% and 70% of the labour force under 18 might never have a proper job. The effect in terms of future training skills, attitudes to work and opportunities for crime and other forms of social disruption is undoubtedly a matter for justifiable concern.'* (*Time Out*, 20.5.83)

'It is extremely serious if Cabinet or Cabinet committee minutes find their way into newspapers. You cannot carry on government on that basis.' (*Daily Telegraph*, 7.12.79)

If, as Mrs Thatcher maintains, unemployment does not cause a growth in crime, perhaps opposition to her economic policies is to blame:

'There are some people who are deeply hostile to everything I believe in because they don't want a free enterprise system. They are out to create anarchy and chaos because they don't want recovery under this system.' (*Sunday Times*, 3.8.80)

Or families are to blame:

'Crime appears to be associated with a range of factors,

such as a record of crime within the family, ineffective supervision and discipline, family discord and weak relationships between parents and children.' (*Hansard*, 18.3.83)

And consumer durables:

'Another factor which has to be taken into account is the general increase in expectations coupled with the increased opportunity for crime arising from the widespread ownership of cars, televisions and other consumer durables.' (*Hansard*, 18.3.83)

Mrs Thatcher admits:

'There is no single or simple cause of crime.' (*Hansard*, 18.3.83.)

But one cause can be isolated:

'The Devil is still with us, recording his successes in the crime figures and in all the other maladies of this society in spite of its material comfort...upholding the law is one area where we would wish the state to be stronger than it is.' (Speech from the pulpit of St Lawrence Jewry, 30.3.78)

How is respect for the law to be restored? What strategy would deal with the Devil and his successes? She once said:

'I would like to see the birch come back. I think it's more important that the public should be protected than to worry about people saying we are putting the clock back.' (*Sunday People*, 23.4.61)

And:

'Today, in spite of the work of the churches, I suspect that only a minority acknowledge the authority of God in their lives. Perhaps that is why we have turned to the state to do so many things which in the past were the prerogative of the family; why crimes of violence are increasing ...' (Speech from the pulpit of St Lawrence Jewry, 4.3.81)

'I think the cane has a place in the training of children.'
(*Sunday Pictorial*, 30.7.61)

And, although she is in favour of capital punishment, Mrs Thatcher claims:

'I don't want hanging used a lot.' (Radio Manchester, 17.9.78)

More police on better pay is a top priority:

'The battle against crime will be pursued with relentless vigour and total commitment...that is why the first action of the new Government was to implement immediately and in full the recommendations of the Edmund Davies report on police pay. That was an earnest of our intention to back the police in their fight against crime.' (*Hansard*, 15.5.79)

Between 1979 and 1983 the number of police in England and Wales increased by 11,850. In the same period, police pay rose by 86.3%. Nurses pay rose by 58% and teachers' by 60%. The policing of England and Wales cost the taxpayer £2,129 million in 1981–2. This figure went up to £2,445 million the following year.
   More weapons are another priority:

'My Right Honourable friend the Home Secretary endorsed the use of CS gas on Merseyside. We are now considering what other equipment the police may need. The use of water cannon is certainly not ruled out.' (*Hansard*, 9.7.81)

Fourteen of Britain's police forces now have stocks of plastic bullets, already used in Northern Ireland.

'Any request from the police for more weapons or weapons

'I am always prepared to exercise penitence ... [laughter] ... This is not a laughing matter.' (*Hansard*, 22.7.82)

🔈 GOOD NEWS

71

'In every urban area there is a large minority of people who are not fit for salvage ... the only way to protect society is, quite frankly, by harrassing these people so that they are too afraid to commit crime.' (Basil Griffiths, Vice–Chairman of Police Federation, *Guardian*, 7.10.82)

of a different sort will be sympathetically considered.' (*Hansard*, 7.4.82)

More police, more weapons — and more prisons. Fourteen new prisons are to be built by 1990 at an estimated cost of £256 million. And to deal with young offenders:

'We shall set up more compulsory attendance centres to which the courts can send young hooligans.' (Manifesto, 1983)

'Any country which wants to proceed towards tyranny starts to undermine legal rights...'(*Evening News*, London, 12.10.66)

Changes in the law will make the job of the police easier by giving them more powers.

'The proposals embodied in our Police and Criminal Evidence Bill will help the police to bring criminals to justice. At the same time they will reinforce public support for the police by laying down clear rules for the proper treatment of suspects.' (Manifesto, 1983)

When this Bill becomes law the police will have:
* Power to hold a person for up to four days for questioning on suspicion of a 'serious arrestable offence'.
* The right to deny access to a lawyer for 36 hours.
* Power to stop, search and arrest on 'reasonable suspicion'. 'Reasonable suspicion' is not defined.
* Power to take fingerprints by force, even from ten-year-olds.
* Power to carry out 'intimate body searches' in police custody.
* Power to arrest without warrant if a person refuses to give

their name and address, or on suspicion that the name and address given is false.

* Power to set up roadblocks on the basis of a 'pattern of crime' in an area, and the 'likelihood of a serious arrestable offence' being committed.

'Most people want to reassert the true values of family and society ... our new Criminal Justice Bill will strengthen the powers of the courts and make parents responsible for their children's fines. It underlines once again parental responsibility for restraining their own actions and teaching the virtues of self-discipline that freedom and order can be guaranteed.' (*Hansard*, 4.12.81)

'I hope that MPs will consider that a paramount function of this House is to safeguard civil liberties rather than to think that administrative convenience should take first place in law.' (*Hansard*, 5.2.60)

The Criminal Justice Act became law in May 1983. In dealing with young offenders it allows curfew orders to be imposed between 6pm and 6am for three-month periods. The National Association for the Care and Rehabilitation of Offenders was convinced that this would lead to an increase in custodial sentences for young people.

'The spirit of our nation also includes some clear convictions about such things as fair play, which we regard as almost a religion in itself, and bullying, which we loathe. This sense of fair play is based on ... some moral absolutes which underpin our social and commercial relationships.' (Speech from the Pulpit of St Lawrence Jewry, 4.3.81)

According to Mrs Thatcher the family, the neighbourhood and the nation all need

'rules to enable them to live together harmoniously and the rules must be backed by some kind of authority, however gently and subtly exercised ...' (Ibid.)

73

'We intend freedom and
justice to conquer. Yes, we
do have a creed and we
wish others to share it. But
it is not part of our policy to
impose our beliefs by force
or threat of force.' (Ottawa,
26.9.83)

Years ago, she foresaw the dangers of the increased use of computers in law enforcement:

'I think it time to reassert a right to privacy ... there is a tendency among some politicians to suggest that with the advent of computers this information should be centralised and stored on magnetic tape. They argue this would be time-saving and more efficient. Possibly it would; but other and more important things would be at stake. There would be produced for the first time a personal dossier about each person, on which everything would be recorded. In my view, this would place far too much power in the hands of the state over the individual.' (Speech, Conservative Political Centre, 10.10.68)

Government departments now have 113 million personal files on computers. The Data Protection Bill allows individuals access to some of their files – but information held on traditional paper files will not be available. Police, customs and tax officials will have access to details on social security benefits, driving licences, immigration documents and other personal information, even when no crime has been committed.

Yet Mrs Thatcher is still able to say:

'Today, no less than when we first came to office, we believe what we say, we say what we believe, and have the courage to see it through. And that is why I am convinced that at least George Orwell was wrong. 1984 will be a year of hope and a year of liberty.' (*Daily Telegraph*, 31.12.83)

But:

'We are strengthening the power of the courts and police

and other agencies of the criminal justice system in their efforts to counter crime.' *(Hansard, 29.3.83)*

In 1979 the Home Office *Research Bulletin* reported: *'There are good reasons for doubting whether further increases in police manpower would reduce or contain the level of crime in this country.'*

'We need more police, not less – they carry out their duties magnificently.' *(Hansard, 26.6.81)*

◀DID YOU KNOW?

The number of crimes went up from 2.5 million recorded offences in 1979 to 3 million in 1982. In both years the number of crimes solved was less than a third.

The 1983 figure was marginally better – there were 1% fewer recorded crimes. But this fall follows 10% rises in the previous two years. In the Metropolitan District, where the police force is biggest and most expensive, only 17.2% of crimes are solved.

Home Office research published in April 1984 reported that *'The police force was now up to strength but the recent growth in police manpower had not been accompanied by any reduction in recorded crime or improvement in the clear-up rate ... There was no evidence that more car patrols or policemen on the beat reduced crime'* (Guardian, 23.4.84).

The greatest challenge to Mrs Thatcher's law and order policies were the riots of 1981. The first riot, in Brixton, was sparked off by the Metropolitan District's 'Operation Swamp' – an attempt to clear up crime by 'swamping' the area with extra police. Lord Chief Justice Scarman was brought in to investigate. He reported: *'Operation Swamp was a big mistake.'* There was, he said, *'a strong undercurrent of hostility to the police.'*

'We must try to overcome the mistrust. It must be got rid of and it is important for our children to look upon the police as friends to whom they can turn if they are in trouble.' (Speech, Liverpool, 13.7.81)

Riots broke out in several major cities. Mrs Thatcher said:

'One is naturally anxious to get closer to the causes. In the meantime, however, one's first action must be to uphold the law and support the police ... we congratulate the police on the work they have done.' (*Hansard*, 7.7.81)

The Scarman Report found that many of the roots of the conflict lay in police practice. It also said: '*Racial disadvantage is a fact of current British life. It was, I am equally sure, a significant factor in the causation of the Brixton disorders. Urgent action is needed if it is not to become an endemic, ineradicable disease threatening the very survival of our society ... I have in mind particularly education and unemployment.*'

Under Mrs Thatcher's Government, we have had more police, more crime and the worst riots in living memory.

'The challenge to exercise discipline, to show wisdom and understanding – they call it Thatcherism and I tell you we need more of it.' (Speech, Canadian and Empire Clubs, Toronto, 27.9.83)

When is a War Not a War? – Northern Ireland

'The Government have repeatedly declared that Northern Ireland is part of the United Kingdom and will remain so unless its people and the Parliament at Westminster decide otherwise. This is the law of the land ... it is fundamental to the Government's thinking. It is something to which I am personally deeply committed.' (Speech, Parliament Buildings, Belfast, 5.3.81)

'The point is to try to get genuine initiatives that lead to a reduction in violence in Northern Ireland and also honour guarantees that have been given.' (*Hansard*, 8.11.83)

'Power as a minister doesn't give you power over the people. In the end, it's the people who have power over you.' (*Liverpool Daily Post* 21.2.72)

Labour and Conservative governments alike have attempted to set up constitutional measures to deal with Northern Ireland since 1969, when the army was sent in. None of these measures have proved successful.

Mrs Thatcher states her commitment to maintaining the union with Britain, but the Unionists suspect betrayal in her every move. The Nationalists continue their fight for unity with the South.

Mrs Thatcher's government is no nearer any solutions than its predecessors.

'We all have a common interest in building better working relationships within these islands and within Europe.' (Speech, Parliament Buildings, Belfast, 5.3.81)

Nicholas Scott, Parliamentary Under-Secretary of State for Northern Ireland, spelled out the Government's fears: if the IRA, and Sinn Fein, were successful in ousting British rule from Northern Ireland, *'Europe would then be faced with an offshore centre for subversion that would not be dissimilar from what the United States and the northern parts of Latin America have endured from Cuba in the last 20 years'* (*The Uncivil Wars*, Padraig O'Malley, Blackstaff 1983).

'I understand the tragedy of Northern Ireland. It is a tragedy in which there are a few people who use the gun, murder, explosives and violence to intimidate the civilian population into surrender when they could not persuade them through the ballot box.' (*The Times*, 15.5.81)

In April 1981, just before he died on hunger strike, Bobby Sands became MP for Fermanagh and South Tyrone with 30,492 votes. After Sands' death, Owen Carron won the seat in August 1981 with an increased majority. In 1983 Sinn Feiner Gerry Adams won the seat for West Belfast, ousting the Catholic moderate Gerry Fitt.

'We do not know why support has gone from the constitutional republican parties to the other parties. That is a deep question.' (*Hansard*, 8.11.83)

'You may chain a man but you cannot chain his mind. You may enslave a man but you cannot conquer his spirit ... but the day comes when the anger and the frustration of the people is so great that force will not contain it. Then the edifice cracks and the mortar crumbles.' (Speech, Berlin, 29.10.82)

Mrs Thatcher understands resistance to communist regimes but has no sympathy for those who resist western governments.

In 1980 and 1981, there were hunger strikes by republican prisoners.

'Faced with their discredited cause the men of violence have chosen in recent months to play what may well be their last card. They have turned their violence against themselves through the hunger strike to death. They seek to work on the most basic of human emotions, pity, as a means of tension and stoking up the fires of bitterness and hatred. In doing so the IRA have put the Catholic community on the rack ... the Government is not prepared to legitimise their cause by word or deed ... these men deny democracy everywhere.' (Speech, Stormont Castle, Belfast, 28.5.81)

'I look forward with great confidence to another period of Convervative government. At the end of that period we shall be approaching our goal ... the goal of a country in which "jam today" is actually on the menu.' (Speech, Convervative Central Council, 22.3.80)

In the past, the Tories have conceded to the demands of hunger strikers in Northern Ireland. During such a protest in 1972, William Whitelaw, then Secretary of State for Northern Ireland, granted special category status for political prisoners and the hunger strike ended before anyone died. This status was removed in 1975, and all prisoners were classified as criminals.

The 1981 hunger strike centered on a list of demands: the restoration of lost remission, free association, the right to wear one's own clothes, to do no prison work, and have educational facilities, regular visits and parcels.

'What the hunger strikers are asking for – let us not mince our words – is political status by easy stages. They cannot have it.' (*Hansard*, 14.5.81)

Ten men died. Since the hunger strike ended the demands have been partially met.

As long as it isn't she who is seen as the oppressor, Mrs Thatcher finds the political struggle of an oppressed people moving. She was inspired by the Polish people.

'There is such a thing as
faith that moves mountains.
I have that faith.' (*The
Times*, 25.3.75)

'Their longing and their struggle for freedom have kindled new hope in their country and all over Western Europe. More than that, they have reminded us in the West of the precious quality of our own freedom. They know what it is like to live without it ... Sooner or later the oppressors will understand that they cannot impose their will upon men and women who ask only that Poland may truly represent the indomitable spirit of the Polish people.' ('Let Poland be Poland' TV Broadcast, 31.1.82)

And:

'I welcome the release of the brave Polish partiot Lech Walesa.' (Lord Mayor's Banquet, 15.11.82)

Lech Walesa said:

'Bobby Sands was a great man who sacrificed his life for his struggle.' (CIS report, 1981)

DID YOU KNOW? 🡒 'In this country one is still innocent until proved guilty.' (*Hansard*, 10.3.81)

In 1983 Mrs Thatcher spoke about the 'narrow and cowardly egotism' of terrorists and said they were

'bolstered by the knowledge that ... tolerant laws of the community based on freedom and justice will ensure a fair trial.' (Speech, British Jewish Community, 21.7.83)

During the Thatcher administration, 400 people have been charged on the uncorroborated evidence of informers in Northern Ireland. In January 1984, 202 people were being held on remand on charges arising from evidence of informers. James Prior told the House that half a million pounds had been spent on informers in the five years up to 1983.

Accused of crimes themselves, 15 informers were granted immunity between 1981–3. Although there is no such thing as political status in Northern Ireland, there are cases defined as 'scheduled offences'. These are politically motivated offences. All such cases are tried in Diplock Courts where there is a judge, but no jury. The Attorney General's recommendations are that in 'supergrass' trials the judge must warn the jury that they may convict but it is dangerous to do so unless the evidence is corroborated. He also says, '*A precisely similar rule applies where a judge is trying a case without a jury. The judge must warn himself*' (Hansard, 24.10.83).

On the evidence of an informer, Charles McCormick was jailed for 20 years on charges including armed robbery and other violent crimes. The Judge, Mr Justice Murray, said: '*It would be highly dangerous and wrong to convict the accused ... unless evidence is supported by clear and compelling corroboration*' (Daily Telegraph, 13.1.84). McCormick successfully appealed against his sentence in January 1984.

Charles McCormick is a former member of the Royal Ulster Constabulary special branch and had been a policeman for 22 years.

Mrs Thatcher says:

'I have full confidence in the judiciary which is independent of politics and must remain so.' (Hansard, 1.12.83)

'The police and army fully accept their duty to operate solely within the law and to act in such a way which wins the support of the whole community.' (Speech, Parliament Buildings, Belfast, 5.3.81)

'We have great confidence in the RUC, UDR and our

'I see some signs that our people are ready to make the tough choice – to follow the harder road.' (*Daily Mirror*, 20.9.75)

armed forces. I pay tribute to the excellent way in which they discharge their duties.' (*Hansard*, 18.11.82)

In December 1982, two young men, Roddy Carroll and Saemus Grew, were on their way home from a funeral. They were followed by members of the security forces in plain clothes who suspected the two men of being members of the Irish National Liberation Army. Part of their journey took them over the border into Southern Ireland. On their return to the North, their car was stopped and both men were killed. Carroll was shot 15 times and Grew four; they were both unarmed. During the trial it emerged that the under-cover security men had crossed the border illegally – the British Ambassador in Dublin had to apologise to the Irish government.

'There is no such thing as political murder.' (Speech, Parliament Buildings, Belfast 5.3.81)

The policeman who fired the shots was acquitted.

'There is still one dark side to this bright industrial renaissance. I refer to unemployment.' (Speech, Conservative Students' Conference, 6.4.84)

'The people of Northern Ireland have endured great hardships ... the impact of the recession is reflected in falling output and rising unemployment, even more acutely in Northern Ireland than elsewhere in the United Kingdom. I know ... the cost in human terms – the waste of resources and the sense of frustration of those who cannot find a job. The decline must be arrested.' (Ibid.)

An EEC report in April 1984 listed the poorest regions of Europe, Calabria headed the list, Northern Ireland came second, followed by Sardinia, Ireland and Merseyside.

'I have seen myself this morning how in spite of everything the people of Belfast are carrying on the commercial and industrial life of the city.' (Speech, Stormont Castle, Belfast, 28.5.81)

'We are engaged in setting free the creative genius of the British people.' (Swansea, 20.7.80)

In April 1979, unemployment in Belfast was 8.5%. In April 1984 it was 17.1%. For Northern Ireland as a whole the numbers of unemployed have more than doubled from 10.1% in April 1979 to 21.5% in April 1984. The worst record is in Strabane where unemployment has gone up from 26.6% to 41%.

'We are committed to the well being of all the people of Northern Ireland.' (Ibid.)

Land of Hope and Glory – Race and Immigration

'Let us resolve to heal the wounds of a divided nation.' (*Daily Telegraph*, 11.10.75)

'It is our hope that those who have come here in the post-war years will no longer be labelled immigrants but have their full place as British citizens with the same rights and responsibilities as the rest of us.' (Speech, Anglo-Asian Conservative Society, 14.7.78)

'The lives of India and Britain are interwoven to a degree rare among nations. In small ways as well as great we are part of each others' history as well as part of each other's present. British interest in India is strong and continuing.' (Speech, Parliament House, Delhi 16.4.81)

'It is cultural and personal contacts that have forged the most direct bonds between our two peoples. You will see restaurants in almost every town doing a roaring trade in Indian food. You will see books about India in every bookshop. Our people are travelling more between our two countries. There was recently a fascinating programme showing beautiful scenes of India and describing it to potential tourists as the holiday of a lifetime.' (Speech, Indo–British Association Dinner, 23.3.82)

The Tory advertising campaign for the June 1983 election sported one poster showing a black man with the caption, 'Labour say he's black, Tories say he's British.' But:

'We do not think people can go on coming in at this present rate. There should be immediate and substantial reduction in the numbers coming in.' (BBC Television, 27.4.77)

'I think people are really rather afraid that this country might be rather swamped by people with a different culture and, you know, the British character has done so much for democracy and law, and done so much throughout the world, that if there is any fear that it might be swamped, people are going to be really rather hostile to those coming in.' (Granada Television, 30.1.78)

'The shouts of the Left cannot drown the voices of anxiety. We have to remove the uncertainty wherever we can. Racial harmony in Great Britain will benefit if some of the doubts about the future are removed, doubts on numbers, doubts on commitments.' (Speech, Young Conservative National Conference, 12.2.78)

Mrs Thatcher exaggerates the number of potential immigrants:

'Britain is no longer an imperial power which can automatically guarantee security and protection to people scattered all over the globe.' (*The Times*, 4.11.76)

And she associates immigrants with Britain's economic ills:

'I explained [to Mrs Ghandi] that the present economic and unemployment situation ruled out any increase in numbers of people admitted to the UK at this time.' (*Hansard*, 5.5.81)

Immigrants will be a drain on resources:

'I want to go into politics and I am doing the thing I love. I would recommend it to anyone who has a passion for what's going on in the world and who wants to do something to make the world a better place.' (*Daily Mail*, 7.6.80)

'I have constantly tried to limit the flow of immigrants . . . a high proportion are young and likely to have families.' (*The Times*, 10.5.78)

In fact, because there are fewer old people in the immigrant community, the community uses fewer resources.

'I heard on the radio the other day that staffing in hotels is frequently from people who are neither British immigrants nor from the EEC. They're still coming in, this is ridiculous.' (*Sunday Times*, 3.8.80)

In the 1979 election the Tories promised changes to cut back immigration:

'Firm immigration control for the future is essential . . . We shall introduce a new British Nationality Act . . . We shall limit entry of parents, grandparents and children over 18 to a small number of compassionate cases.' (Manifesto, 1979)

Between 1978 and 1982, more people left the United Kingdom than entered. *'We have got finally to dispose of the lingering notion that Britain is somehow home for all those countries we once ruled,'* said Timothy Raison, the minister responsible for the Nationality Bill (*The Times*, 9.10.80).

The Bill became a fully operational Act on 1 January 1983. British nationality is now divided into five categories; only full British citizens are free of immigration controls and have a right to settle in the country. All other categories are subject to controls. The Act also removed the automatic right of Commonwealth citizens to register as British. After 1 January 1983, children born in the United Kingdom do not become citizens unless one of their parents is British or settled in Britain.

'*Far too much money is spent on these* [Asian] *families. The more you do for these people, the more they expect.'* (Tory Councillor Graham Ling, *Asian Times*, 25.11.83)

'*We went wanging down there* [Southall]*, jumped out of the van and just started fighting . . . it was a great day out fighting the Pakis. It ought to be an annual fixture. I thoroughly enjoyed myself.'* (London policeman quoted in Policy Studies Institute Report, 1983)

87

Louis Providence, from St Vincent, West Indies, had lived in England for 20 years. He served in the Royal Navy in the Falklands and, on his return home, found a letter from the Home Office Immigration Department. Thanks to the Nationality Act, Louis Providence wasn't British any more; he would have to re-apply for citizenship (at a cost of £70).

In 1980 the immigration rules were changed so that only women born in Britain (or with a parent born here) had the right to be joined by fiancés or husbands. Because the European Court of Human Rights was likely to rule against Britain, the law was changed in 1983 to allow all female British citizens to bring in their husbands and fiancés.

'Control of immigration into Britain is essential if we are to maintain good race relations. Our immigration officials are instructed to carry out their duties in accordance with the law without regard to race, colour or religion.' (Speech, Parliament House, Delhi, 16.4.81)

Husbands and fiancés are indeed allowed into the country, but only if they have satisfied the immigration authorities that the 'primary purpose' of their marriage is not to gain admission to Britain. A marriage might be 'genuine' and still a fiancé or husband can be turned away if the immigration authorities are not convinced. In the last four months of 1983, 40 husbands and 230 fiancés from the Indian sub-continent were refused entry – half of the husbands and 190 fiancés under the 'primary purpose rule'.

DID YOU KNOW? ☛ **'We live in the age of the Jumbo jet. Millions of people visit Britain each year, including last year 190,000 Indians. Inevitably, when such large numbers are involved, a few people try to enter illegally and inevitably a few are therefore turned back ... The Government, like its predecessors, is committed to creating a just and racially harmonious**

'When we go to the country we shall, I believe, be able to say: "We have pointed the way, we have set our people at long last on the right path".' (*Sunday Express*, 23.3.80)

society. We are committed to ensuring that there are equal opportunities for all our people regardless of their race, background or national origin. We shall stick to that commitment.' (Ibid.)

Deportations have reached 2,000 a year. In 1984, Afia Begum and her three-year-old-daughter will be included in the statistics. In 1982 Afia Begum applied to join her husband in Britain. Just before she arrived, he was killed in a fire and permission to stay was withdrawn. She was only allowed in to the country to settle her husband's affairs. Most of her family are in Britain. A dawn raid by immigration officials and police ended her stay. She was deported.

Of the deportation orders made in 1983, 1,591 were for administrative reasons, not crimes. Some of these people will have spent some time – possibly months – in jail.

'We shall invoke the full force of the law to end the present wave of brutal attacks by young thugs on minority communities.' (Speech, Anglo-Asian Conservative Society, 14.7.78)

The Home Office Report on Racial Attacks (November 1981) found that *'the incidence of victimisation has been much higher for the ethnic minority populations. The rate for blacks was over 36 times that for white people.'* In the category 'other serious offences', 72% of victims were black or Asian. During a two month study in 13 police areas, racially motivated attacks 'occurred on a significant scale'. Asians were 50 times more likely to be victims of attacks than white people.

'The growth of the black community would turn cities into citadels of urban terrorism.' (Enoch Powell, *Morning Star*, 12.7.80)

According to Mrs Thatcher:

'The only way to succeed in maintaining and securing tolerance for all minority groups in this country is by holding out the clear prospect of an end to immigration.' (*Daily Telegraph*, 25.3.77)

In 1982 the Metropolitan Police published alarmist crime statistics, broken down into racial groups. 'Mugging' became an emotive word associated with black crime. 'Mugging' — robbery and violent theft — amounted to less than 1% of all recorded serious crime in the Metropolitan area.

'[In the police] it is normal, automatic and habitual to refer to black people as "coons" and "niggers".' (Policy Studies Institute, 1983)

In April 1981, rioting broke out in Brixton, London, an area with a large immigrant population. Lord Scarman, who headed the subsequent report on the riots, said they were sparked off by *'unlawful and, in particular, racially prejudiced conduct by some of our police officers.'*

'My party is very anxious to maintain good relations with immigrants.' (*Daily Telegraph*, 1.9.76)

But Mrs Thatcher also wants to appease the far right in the party. At the Tory Conference in 1983, delegates debated a motion to strengthen immigration laws. The motion called for the repeal of all race relations legislation and an increase in the financial help given to encourage repatriation. The motion (which was defeated) was moved by Harvey Proctor, MP for Billericay. Other Tory MPs have spoken along similar lines. John Carlisle, MP for Luton North, said: *'Black trouble-makers should be sent home even if they were born here'*. (*Daily Mirror*, 29.4.81).

Tougher vetting measures for members of the Tory Party were announced by Party Chairman John Gummer after a

Young Conservatives' report exposed the growing number of extreme right-wingers. Tory Action, an extreme right-wing group, claimed to have links with twenty Tory MPs. Right-wing extremism in the Party was exposed by BBC's 'Panorama' programme on 30 January 1984. The Tory Party hotly denied the allegations but did not entirely refute that several Tory MPs are involved with groups such as Tory Action.

'There is no racism in the Conservative Party. We believe in equal opportunities for all citizens, whatever their background.' (*Hansard*, 2.2.84)

Red Alert –
Defence

'The way to achieve peace with freedom is to pursue multilateral disarmament so that we can retain our security at very much less expense to the nation.' (*Hansard*, 12.11.81)

Mrs Thatcher has presided over a programme of arming Britain with Cruise and Trident weapon systems. There has been a 23% increase in defence spending since 1979. This is the largest defence budget for twenty years and higher than any other European member of NATO in absolute terms and per head of the population.

'I think the vast majority of people would believe that the independent deterrent of Trident is extremely good value for money.' (*Hansard*, 19.5.81)

Four Trident submarines (carrying 892 warheads) are due to replace the existing four Polaris submarines (carrying 192 warheads) in the 1990s. The origial cost of Trident was to be £5 billion. The latest figure is £8.7 billion. Independent research puts it at £11.5 billion.

'A great many jobs in connection with Trident will come to Britain, particularly at the peak of the programme when there will be about 20,000 jobs.' (*Hansard*, 25.3.82)

'Every Conservative desires peace. The threat to peace comes from Communism which has powerful forces ready to attack anywhere. Communism waits for weakness, it leaves strength alone. Britain must therefore be strong, strong in her arms, strong in her faith, strong in her own way of life.' (Margaret Roberts' election leaflet, 1950)

Senior defence officials told the Commons Public Accounts Committee that the Trident programme was unlikely to create jobs in Britain.

As for the independence of the deterrent, the warheads will be directed to their targets from the Strategic Air Command bunker in Omaha, Nebraska, using American satellite information. There are 96 Cruise missiles at Greenham Common airbase; each one carries the equivalent of 16 Hiroshima atom bombs. There is no 'dual key' mechanism, which means, in effect, that the Americans alone have ultimate control over the launch of Cruise. Mrs Thatcher argues:

GOOD NEWS ☛ **'It would require the decision of both the President of the United States and the current Prime Minister before any such weapons be fired. President Reagan has already made that perfectly clear and has said in the United States that it is tantamount to a veto.'** (*Hansard*, 12.7.83)

The actual consultation procedures for launching cruise were set down in a 1952 communiqué between Winston Churchill and President Truman which says that consultation will be exercised 'time and circumstances permitting'.

'NATO guidelines acknowledge that in the final analysis the decision to use nuclear weapons would remain the prerogative of the government who owns them.' (Chatham House Special Paper, The Royal Institute of International Affairs, 1984)

Cruise is owned by America, but:

'We are very fortunate to have someone else's weapons stationed on our soil to fight those targeted against us.' (*Time*, 16.2.81)

THE FILM TO END ALL FILMS

The most EXPLOSIVE
love story ever

MILTON FRIEDMAN
in association with PENTAGON PRODUCTIONS presents

"GONE WITH
THE WIND"

SCREENPLAY BY   DIRECTED BY   MUSIC BY
KIS JOSEPH   HANK KISSINGER   EDDY HEATH

Winner
of Ten
Academy
Awards

She promised to follow him to the end of the earth.
He promised to organise it!

AN IMF PICTURE   RIGHT RANK INC

Now showing world-wide

'I first became interested in communism from reading about it when I was 16 or 17. The thing which struck me very vividly was the total extinction of all personal liberty. I saw then that they had a world objective – to dominate the world – which they pursued by one means or another. And this obviously never left me. It's not in the back-ground of my mind, but in my bloodstream.' (*Daily Telegraph*, 19.12.83)

Who is winning the Nuclear Arms Race? Opinions differ, but according to the Stockholm Institute for Strategic Studies the USA has 10,000 more warheads than the USSR.

'The United States is contributing massively to the defence of Europe and we should be very grateful.' (*Hansard*, 27.10.83)

Mrs Thatcher doesn't like public opposition to Cruise missiles – particularly the Greenham Common women demonstrators:

'Such protests give the impression to the United States that this country has neither the capacity nor the resolve to defend itself. Such action is contrary to the interests of this country.' (*Hansard*, 16.12.82)

When Ronald Reagan was elected President of the United States in 1980, Mrs Thatcher was delighted:

'The election of a man committed to the cause of freedom and the renewal of America's strength has given encouragement to all those who love liberty.' (Speech, United Nations, 28.2.81)

'Freedom will be our battle cry and the individual will be our watchword. Every child knows the story of Little Red Riding Hood and what happened to her in her grandmother's cottage in the forest. Despite the new look of these Communist parties, despite the softness of their voices, we should be on the watch for the teeth and the appetite of the wolf.' (*Morning Star*, 26.5.76)

Russia and Communism are the enemies of justice, peace and freedom:

'They put guns before butter while we put everything before guns.' (Speech, Kensington Town Hall, 20.1.76)

'Remember that poem of Kipling's – "The Female of the Species is More Deadly than the Male"? No man is as tough as a woman in defence of his children. I think women are more interested in the long term future than men because they are thinking about the world in which their children will live.' (*Daily Mail*, 18.11.76)

DID YOU KNOW? ☛

'We' spend more on defence than anything else bar the social security budget.

'My job is to stop Britain going red.' (*The Times*, 3.11.77)

'She [USSR] has put enormous resources into research and technology for all weapons of destruction in preference to raising the living standards of her own society.' (*Hansard*, 13.2.81)

Funds for similar research under the Conservative Government have gone up from £880 million in 1977–8 to £1668 million in 1982–3.

Some of the presents received by Ronald Reagan in 1982:
* From the Queen, three eighteenth–century Worcester dishes (value $9,000).
* From the Duke of Edinburgh, an autographed photograph of himself (value unknown).
* From the Prince and Princess of Wales, a Wedgwood vase (value $2,400).
* From Margaret Thatcher, a music box that plays 'Take a Pair of Sparkling Eyes' (value incalculable).

Mrs Thatcher's special relationship with President Reagan has flourished:

'I'm a fundamental believer, as is the United States, in democracy. We never cease to say how marvellous freedom and justice are and how wonderful it is to live within freedom and justice.' (BBC World Service, 30.10.83)

In October 1983 the United States invaded Grenada. Mrs Thatcher objected:

'Western democracies try to extend our beliefs not by force but by persuasion. You do not cross into an independent country. Communism, oppression, yes, I hate it. There are many peoples in countries of the world who would love to be free of it. That doesn't mean we can just walk into them and say, "You're free," I'm afraid.' (Ibid.)

But on the same programme she said:

'I see little point in arguing about it. The people of Grenada will be delighted to be free of an oppressive rule, so would many people around the world be delighted to be free of oppressive communism.' (Ibid.)

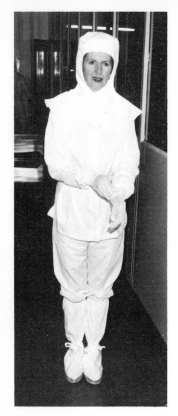

'We may not like them [the Russians] **but we have to live with them on the same planet.'** (*Daily Mail*, 7.11.83)

And finally:

'His [Reagan's] perspective is one of regional security. It justifies him crossing into Grenada. He has relieved that country of communism.' (Ibid.)

'The Americans can rely on me absolutely in defence and in everything in which I believe.' (*Daily Mail*, 7.11.83)

The breach was healed:

'Friends like families differ at times. But nothing alters the basic truths – that the United States is our ultimate defensive shield, the guarantor of Western freedom and the best hope for the world's oppressed. To that conviction we hold. We are confident that any difference which may occur will always be infinitely less important than the purposes and loyalties that bind us together.' (Lord Mayor's Banquet, 14.11.83)

When all is said and done:

'The United States and Britain are allies. We would always have to accept any advice the United States gave us. Indeed it follows that we would not be free to accept or reject the advice of the United States. The United States is the final guarantor of freedom in Europe.' (*Hansard*, 27.10.83)

'By the late 1970s there were enough nuclear weapons in the world to destroy it seven times over.' (*Of Bread and Guns*, Nigel Harris, Pelican 1983)

Mrs Thatcher says:

'Since the last world war there have been 140 wars fought

with ordinary weapons, which are themselves horrific, and nuclear weapons have been a deterrent to war. I therefore believe we should keep them.' (*Hansard*, 15.6.82)

Even though:

'If you look at the prospects of a nuclear war it is totally and utterly horrific.' (*Daily Mail*, 7.11.83)

But would Mrs Thatcher actually use nuclear weapons?

'If necessary, yes.' (*Hansard*, 15.1.81)

'Communism never sleeps, never changes its objectives. Nor must we.' (*Financial Times*, 23.5.79)

Her Finest Hour –
The Falklands War

'If you can't succeed with people at home, then try to impress them with overseas adventures.' (Speech, Conservative Central Council, 8.4.78)

Mrs Thatcher was criticising the Prime Minister, James Callaghan – her words, in retrospect, are ironic.

HEART OF THE MATTER ☞ The Falkland Islands were colonised by the British in 1833. Argentina has claimed them ever since. John Troutbeck, of the Foreign Office, wrote in 1936: *'The difficulty of our position is that our seizure of the Falkland Islands in 1833 was so arbitary a procedure. It is not easy to explain our possession of the islands without showing ourselves up as international bandits.'*

In 1979, the new Conservative Government set about building up its contacts with the ruling military dictatorship in Argentina. That year, the special refugee programme, which provided assistance for people escaping from Argentina who wanted to come to Britain, was scrapped.

Diplomatic relations with Argentina were re-established in February 1980. Six months later, Cecil Parkinson, then Minister for Trade, went on a personal visit to Buenos Aires. He spoke to their Chamber of Commerce: *'We are making industry responsible for its own future, while creat-*

ing the right environment for companies to prosper. We are encouraging competition ... I can only applaud your own efforts in this direction. So you can see just how close Argentina and Britain are in their economic policies' (Daily Mirror, 28.4.82).

The ban on the sale of arms was lifted: *'Over a period of years Argentina has purchased Tigercat, Seacat, Blowpipe and Sea Dart, all of which are British manufactured surface-to-air missiles. The value of sales in the past five years: 1977, £0.7 million; 1978, £4.9 million; 1979, £62.6 million; 1980, £46.7 million; 1981, £12.5 million'* (Hansard, 20.4.82).

Argentina was still pressing her claims. In November 1980, Nicholas Ridley visited the Falkland Islands to discuss proposals for a lease-back scheme – the Islands would become Argentinian but would be leased back to Britain.

The status of the islanders themselves was also in question, as the Government's changes in the nationality laws were debated in Parliament. Lord Trefgarne, junior minister at the Foreign Office, said: *'However strong the affection, the fact remains that the Falklands are not and never have been part of the United Kingdom'* (House of Lords, 28.7.81). As a result, 400 of the 1,800 islanders became British Dependent Territories Citizens, which gave them no right to enter or live in Britain.

The following year the Government decided that HMS Endurance would be withdrawn from her patrols in the Falklands area. James Callaghan warned Margaret Thatcher: *'To withdraw HMS Endurance is an error that could have grave consequences.'* She defended the decision:

'Other claims on the defence budget should have greater priority.' (Hansard, 9.2.82)

'The Falkland Islands are British, the Falkland Islanders are British. They are our own people. With the Falkland Islanders it is family.' (Speech, Conservative Women's Conference, 26.5.82)

'I tend to look at things more logically than do my colleagues. They come eventually [to my point of view] because there aren't any other ways to go.'
(French television, 3.80)

The subsequent inquiry into events – the 1983 Franks Report – concluded: *'It was inadvisable for the Government to announce a decision to withdraw HMS Endurance.'* It looked as though Britain was no longer prepared to defend the islands.

The Argentines invaded the Falkland Islands on Friday 2 April. On Saturday 3 April the House of Commons met in special session. Margaret Thatcher opened the debate:

'The House meets this Saturday to respond to a situation of great gravity. We are here because for the first time for many years, British sovereign territory has been invaded... We have absolutely no doubt about our sovereignty which has been continuous since 1833.' (*Hansard*, 3.4.82)

As the House of Commons debated the prospect of war, the first ships of the British fleet were already on their way to the South Atlantic – beside the vast support network, British military strength would eventually number 62 surface warships, 6 submarines, 42 aircraft and 200 helicopters.

What would this vast armada be expected to do? Margaret Thatcher said:

'I cannot foretell what orders the task force will receive as it proceeds. That will depend on the situation at the time. Meanwhile we hope that our continuing diplomatic efforts by our many friends will be met with success.' (*Hansard*, 3.4.82)

John Nott wasn't so sure: *'We intend to solve the problem and we shall try to solve it continuingly by diplomatic means, but if that fails, and it will probably do so, we shall have no choice but to press forward with our plans.'* (*Hansard*, 3.4.82)

Enoch Powell challenged Mrs Thatcher: *'The Prime Minister shortly after she came into office received a soubriquet as the "Iron Lady". It arose in the context of remarks she made about defence against the Soviet Union and its allies; but there is no reason to suppose that the Right Honourable Lady did not welcome and indeed take pride in that description. In the next week or two this House, the nation and the Right Honourable Lady herself will learn of what metal she is made.'* (Hansard, 3.4.82)

Having sent the British fleet, would Mrs Thatcher use it? As the weeks passed the question became more acute. Within the War Cabinet – Margaret Thatcher, William Whitelaw, Cecil Parkinson, John Nott and Francis Pym – there were differences of opinion. Francis Pym, Foreign Secretary, told the House: *'I am doing everything I can to try to achieve a peaceful settlement. It has at times, sadly, been necessary to resort to military means. Nobody wants that to happen, but we cannot exclude that possibility. But I will exclude it so long as negotiations are in play'* (Hansard, 21.4.82).

He had to return to the chamber later the same day and correct himself: *'I understand there may have been some misunderstanding. I think I made it clear throughout the exchanges that however hard I was trying to achieve a peaceful settlement the use of force could not at any stage be ruled out'* (Hansard, 21.4.82).

Mrs Thatcher emphasised this position the next day:

'I confirm what my Right Honourable friend, the Foreign Secretary, said yesterday: that while we are making every effort to secure a peaceful settlement, the use of force cannot be ruled out. The process of negotiations could go on endlessly.' (Hansard. 22.4.82)

'I was on the Jimmy Young show, he played an Andy Williams song for me. He knows I like Andy Williams and the song was "The Other Side of Me". Well, there are two sides of me – the informal, friendly me and the Iron Touch, the Iron Lady.' (*Daily Mail*, 3.5.80)

On 26 April she told the House:

'Time is short because of the weather conditions, the distance from home and because the task force is now approaching the Islands. We shall have greater chances of a peaceful settlement if we bring military pressure to bear.' (*Hansard*, 26.4.82)

That night, Mrs Thatcher said on television:

'I had the winter at the back of my mind. The winter; what will the winter do? The wind, the cold. Down in South Georgia the ice, what will it do? It beat Napoleon at Moscow.' (*Daily Express*, 26.7.82)

'Some people say "don't use force while negotiations are continuing". It is an easy argument. It enables them to carry on and on with negotiations. In the meantime it will get more and more difficult for us to use a military option 8,000 miles from home at the onset of winter in very terrible weather, gales and freezing.' (BBC Television, 26.4.82)

On 30 April a Total Exclusion Zone was declared around the Falklands; any Argentine ship or aircraft that came within 200 miles of the islands would be attacked.

That night a British Vulcan bomber took off from Ascension Island and on the morning of Saturday 1 May dropped its 1,000lb bombs on Stanley airstrip (with only one direct hit). The plan was to prevent the Argentines flying supplies to support their troops on the ground. Later that day Francis Pym, en route to Washington for more talks with General Haig, Britain's mediator with the Argentines, told news reporters that the bombing was intended to '*concentrate Argentine minds*' on the need for a peaceful settlement. '*No further military action is envisaged for the moment other than making the Total Exclusion Zone secure*' (*The Times*, 4.5.82).

But as he spoke, HMS Conqueror, a nuclear-powered British submarine, had the Argentine cruiser General Belgrano in her sights.

The Belgrano was sunk on Sunday 2 May, with the loss of 368 of her crew.

Who took the decision to sink her? The submarine commander, Wreford-Brown, told the press: *'The decision to attack was taken at HQ* [in Northwood, Middlesex]' (*Aberdeen Press and Journal*, 5.7.82).

Rear-Admiral 'Sandy' Woodward, commander of the Task Force in the South Atlantic, said: *'I sought a major change in the Rules of Engagement to enable the Conqueror to attack Belgrano outside the exclusion zone. This was achieved in remarkably short order, reputedly in the entrance porch at Chequers'* (Lecture, Royal United Services Institute, 20.10.82).

Why did the war cabinet decide to sink the Belgrano? John Nott said she was *'close to the total exclusion zone and was closing in on elements of our task force which was only hours away'* (*Hansard*, 4.5.82).

No she wasn't. Peter Blaker, Minister of State for Defence admitted: *'At the moment it was torpedoed the General Belgrano was on a course of 280 degrees'* (*Hansard*, 29.11.82) – that is, west-north-west, heading towards the South American mainland and away from the Falklands and the task force.

The Belgrano, and the rest of the Argentine fleet, had been called back to port. Signals were sent out on Saturday 1 May – the day before she was torpedoed – and again on Sunday 2 May, at 1.19 am. And all communications between the Argentine military were being decoded at GCHQ in Cheltenham.

H. E. Bonzo, captain of the Belgrano, survived: *'I thought that a Total Exclusion Zone must mean that if you were in it*

'The supreme task of modern statesmanship is the prevention of war.'
(Speech, United Nations, 28.2.81)

➤ **DID YOU KNOW?**

you got shot at. If you were not in it, you did not get shot at. But if you are going to be shot at in any case, then, tell me, why have a Total Exclusion Zone at all?' (*The Sinking of the Belgrano*, Rice and Gavshon, Secker & Warburg 1984)

Before the sinking of the Belgrano, President Belaunde of Peru had mediated between President Galtieri, General Haig and Francis Pym. Belaunde was so sure that a peaceful settlement was about to be reached that he held a televised press conference on the afternoon of Sunday 2 May to announce that peace was on hand *'this very night'*.

While Galtieri and his junta were meeting that evening, news came through of the sinking of the Belgrano. The peace negotiations were scuppered. Mrs Thatcher said:

'The next stage of the negotiations was based on proposals originally advanced by President Belaunde of Peru and modified in consultations between him and Mr Haig. As my Right Honourable friend [Mr Pym] informed the House on 7 May, Britain was willing to accept these, the fifth set of proposals for an interim settlement. They could have led to an almost immediate ceasefire. But again it was Argentina who rejected them.' (*Hansard*, 20.5.82)

Argentina did reject these proposals – *after* Britain sank the Belgrano.

On 4 May, HMS Sheffield was sunk – 21 lives were lost. Inevitably, hostilities escalated and the toll of dead and wounded mounted up on both sides. Argentina surrendered on 14 June.

'We thank you all: those who are here; the many who, for reasons of space, could not be here; the 777 valiant young men who were wounded; the 255 who gave their lives and whose memory will be honoured forever... The spectacle of bold young Britons fighting for great principles and a just

cause, lifted the nation. Doubts and hesitation were replaced by confidence and pride that our younger generation too could write a glorious chapter in the history of liberty.' (Speech, Salute to the Task Force Luncheon, 12.10.82)

Not everyone agreed: *'I am proud of my son, but not proud of the fact that he died for his country in a war which was not necessary. I accept that it's a serviceman's duty to fight. But in a futile situation like this I think it's evil to put men's lives at risk when negotiations around a table can save so much heartbreak'* (Mother of Mark Sambles, killed on HMS Glamorgan, *Bridport News*, 18.6.82).

Before the war the Government's popularity had been at an all-time low. In the polls, the Conservatives had had the

'The Queen is a much more important person than I. As I have said before, I am from a very ordinary background.' (*Daily Telegraph*, 25.9.75)

'I know how strongly many people feel that the case for our country is not being put with sufficient vigour on certain – I do not say all – BBC programmes. It is our great pride that the British media is free. But we expect the case for freedom to be put by those who are responsible for doing so' (11.5.82).

The previous night, BBC's 'Panorama' programme had interviewed four MPs – two Labour, two Conservative – who were opposed to the Falklands war.

support of 27.5% of the electorate in January; it was 45% in June. Margaret Thatcher had good cause to 'Rejoice! Rejoice!'

'Our country has won a great victory and we are entitled to be proud. This nation had the resolution to do what it knew had to be done – to do what it knew was right. We fought to show that aggression does not pay and that the robber cannot be allowed to get away with his swag ... When the demands of war and the danger to our people calls us to arms – then we British are as we have always been – competent, courageous and resolute. When called to arms – ah, that's the problem. Why does it need a war to bring out our qualities and reassert our pride? Why do we have to be invaded before we throw aside our selfish aims and begin to work together as only we can work together and achieve as only we can achieve? That really is the challenge we face today. We have to see that the spirit of the South Atlantic – the real spirit of Britain – is kindled not only by war but can now be fired by peace.' (Speech, Conservative Rally, Cheltenham, 3.7.82)

She went on to attack the train drivers – then on strike – for 'misunderstanding the new mood of the nation', and warned the health workers and nurses about their pay claim:

'We can't avoid one unchallengable truth. The Government has no money of its own. All that it has it takes in taxes or borrows at interest. It's all of you – everyone here – that pays.' (Ibid.)

Kevin McNamara MP estimated the cost of maintaining the garrison on the Falklands, including men, ships, planes and provisioning to be £684 million per year (£380,000 per islander). And the cost for the year of the war is now estimated to be £1,600 million.

When hostilities began, the Government severed all diplomatic and financial links with Argentina.

'Others say we must not put at risk our investments and interests in Latin America; that trade and commerce are too important to us to put in jeopardy some of the valuable markets of the world. But what would the islanders under the heel of the invader say to that?' (Speech, Conservative Women's Conference, 26.5.82)

Within six months of the war ending, British bank loans to Argentina were already being renegotiated.

'With the support of the International Monetary Fund, negotiations have been taking place on two loans to be provided by a group of international banks, including British banks.' (*Hansard*, 20.12.82)

And what had the whole episode meant to Margaret Thatcher?

'When you've spent half your political life dealing with humdrum issues like the environment, it's exciting to have a real crisis on your hands.' (Speech, Scottish Conservative Party Conference, 14.5.82)

'I cannot easily foresee the time when we have a woman Minister of Defence. But it would give me enormous joy to have the navy singing "There is Nothing Like a Dame".' (Speech, 'Women and Power' conference, 24.4.75)

Ladies First –

Women

'Many women have the opportunities but do not use them ... or are too easily contented with the job that they're doing and do not necessarily make the effort to climb the tree ... sometimes it's thought to be unfeminine. It isn't at all, you know.' (BBC World Service, 2.3.84)

'It is noticeable that many of the suffragettes were very womanly.' (Speech, Institution of Electrical Engineers, 26.7.82)

'It is possible, in my view, for a woman to run a home and continue with her career provided two conditions are fulfilled. First, her husband must be in sympathy with her wish to do another job. Secondly, where there is a young family, the joint incomes of husband and wife must be sufficient to employ a first-class nanny–housekeeper to look after things in the wife's absence. The second is the key of the whole plan.' (*Evening News*, London, 25.2.60)

'If we couldn't afford to have resident help in the home, I would give up my career tomorrow.' (*Daily Telegraph*, 3.12.68)

A married woman who wants to have a full-time job needs, according to Mrs Thatcher, to be:

'... extremely well organised. She has to be able to deal with domestic affairs quickly, make up her mind about household menus and shopping lists. And if she also has children there has to be someone responsible at home to care for them, whether it's a mother-in-law, a sister or a nanny.' (*Sunday Express*, 16.1.72)

The Equal Opportunities Commission estimated that the demand for nursery places far outstrips the supply. Finding childcare is especially difficult for single parents. Over

100,000 children go to childminders. A childminder earns about £22 a week. A full-time live-in nanny's salary is £60 – tax and National Insurance are paid by the employer.

'I still do the cooking myself . . . rush in, peel the vegetables, put the roast in, all before I take off my hat. There are all sorts of emergencies that women at home all day build up into mountains. But a job, outside interests, keep the emergencies fairly well in proportion.' (*Daily Telegraph*, 18.3.66)

In 1981, when the latest figures were collected, 6% of mothers with children under five had full-time jobs; 18% had part-time jobs. Only 15% of all women with children had full-time work. One in eight families is headed by a single parent – in almost all cases, a woman.

'I think they [feminists] **have become far too strident and have done damage to the cause of women by making us out to be something we're not. You get on because you have the right talents.'** (*The Times*, 10.5.78)

'I am absolutely satisified that there is nothing more you can do by changing the law to do away with discrimination. After all, I don't think there's been a great deal of discrimination against women for years.' (Thames Television, 6.1.81)

* Unemployment for women has trebled since 1979.
* Three-quarters of low-paid workers are women.
* In 1979, women earned 59% of men's earnings in manual jobs. In 1983, they earned 61.2% of a man's wage.
* Two out of five women workers are employed part-time. One in ten men works part-time.

'I loved my mother dearly, but after I was 15 we had nothing more to say to each other. It wasn't her fault. She was weighed down by the home, always being in the home.' (*Daily Express*, 17.4.61)

'I've always had an English nanny, otherwise I'd never have left the children happily.' (*Newcastle Journal*, 3.12.68)

'I don't notice that I'm a woman. I regard myself as the Prime Minister.' (*Daily Mirror*, 1.3.80)

* The right to take maternity leave has been eroded by the 1980 Employment Protection Act.

Unemployment benefit is paid to people who are 'available for work.' Since 1982, part of the availability test includes a form asking one to prove that arrangements are made for the care of children and dependants.

'The trouble is that there are still not as many of us who have made the grade as men. Therefore we stand out more conspicuously.' (*Daily Telegraph*, 6.5.66)

There are 72 High Court judges; three are women. Women make up almost 50% of all secondary-school teachers; 16.3% are headmistresses. Women make up only 22% of the medical profession. One half of all female workers are in servicing jobs — catering, cleaning, nursing, teaching.

When the Conservatives lost the 1974 general election, Mrs Thatcher found herself out of office:

DID YOU KNOW? ☞

'It's easier for a woman than a man to give up his power because you are not so lost. A woman can fill the time spring-cleaning the house.' (*Daily Mail*, 9.3.74)

'One does wish there were women in Parliament because then one would be less conspicuous oneself. I'd like to get on with the job without being in the limelight all the time.' (*Sunday Express*, 16.1.72)

'I think Women's Lib came on the scene rather after I did. I don't know much about them, but I reckon I know a lot about men and women.' (*Sun*, 16.7.75)

Of the 395 Tory MPs in Parliament, 14 are women. There is only one woman in the Cabinet — Margaret Thatcher.

'The battle for women's rights has been largely won. The days when they were demanded and discussed in strident tones should be gone forever. And I hope they are. I hated those strident tones you hear from some "Women's Libbers".' (Speech, Institution of Electrical Engineers, 26.7.82)

'The Queen is most anxious to enlist everyone who can speak or write to join in checking this mad, wicked folly of 'Woman's Rights' with all its attendant horrors...' (Queen Victoria, in a letter dated 1870)

'I was asked whether I was trying to restore Victorian values. I said straight out I was. And I am.' (Speech, British Jewish Community, 21.7.83)

Let Our Children Grow Tall – The Family

'One of the most revealing things about the rhetoric of the Left is the almost total absence of any reference to the family. Yet the family is the basic unit of our society. It is within the family that the next generation is nurtured.' (*The Times*, 17.10.81)

'Let our children grow tall – and some taller than others.' (Speech, Institute of Socio-Economic Studies, 16.9.75)

But families are not doing well under Mrs Thatcher's Government. In 1979 there were 923,143 children in families on the poverty line – in 1982 there was 1.7 million. Unemployment among 16-year-olds has almost doubled for girls and has trebled for boys.

'Child benefit will be increased. This increase to its highest ever real value is evidence of our commitment to the family.' (*Hansard*, 28.6.83)

Between 1979 and 1983 child benefit went up from £4 to £6.50 per week, a rise worth ten pence after allowing for inflation.

'What is the real driving force of society? It is the desire for the individual to do the best for himself and his family. How is society improved? By millions of people resolving that they will give their children a better life than they have had themselves.' (Speech, Cardiff, 16.4.79)

However:

'This party is very much in favour of the family but that does not mean arguing for every single benefit to be increased.' (*Hansard*, 17.1.80)

VITAL STATISTIC ☛ Families on unemployment benefits have lost about £4.65 in real terms since 1979. Cuts in housing benefits mean that many families on low incomes will have lost up to £7.28 a week by the end of 1984.

'We believe that the individual citizen should have more encouragement to provide for his own future, that it should always pay to work, that a sound family life lies at the heart of a healthy society.' (*The Right Approach*, Conservative Party Central Office, 1976)

Families on three times average earnings (£25,000) were 11% better off in 1984 than in 1979. At five times average earnings (£40,000), they were 22% better off.

'Let us remember that we are a nation and that a nation is an extended family ... Let us do all in our power to see one another's point of view and to widen the common ground on which we stand.' (*Daily Telegraph*, 13.10.78)

'Somebody said – or if they didn't they should have – life does change, that is what makes it different from death.' (Speech, Canada, 26.9.83)

'In family matters today there are some very disquieting features. One in ten marriages is expected to break down after five years and one in three after thirty years.' (Speech, Institution of Electrical Engineers, 26.7.82)

In 1979, 163,861 people filed for divorce. In 1982 the number had increased to 174,373.

'The number of girls who conceived children under the age

'My policies are based not on some economic theory but on things I and millions like me were brought up with. An honest day's work for an honest day's pay; live within your means; put by a nest egg for a rainy day; pay your bills on time; support the police.' (*News of the World*, 20.9.81)

of 16 has risen from 6,600 in 1970 to 8,100 in 1979.' (Ibid.)

'*In 1975 there were 11.01 pregnancies per 1,000 fifteen-year-olds. In 1982 there were 9.85.*' (*Hansard*, 8.11.83) This drop corresponds with the 1975 DHSS guidelines to doctors that girls under 16 should be able to get contraception without parental consent. Mrs Thatcher supports the campaign to reverse these guidelines.

'**The Government itself endorses fully the wish to uphold and strengthen the family and parental responsibility and has every sympathy with the feelings which lie behind the points which have been made.**' (*Medical News*, 5.4.84)

The British Medical Association is strongly against any change in the DHSS directive.

'**Children have been encouraged to grow up faster and to see themselves as independent of parents. Parents have been told by self-appointed experts that their duties to each other and to their children should be balanced by more emphasis on self-fulfillment. In other words we have seen the birth of the permissive society. Has this benefitted women? Far from it. Women know that society is founded on dignity, reticence and discipline. We know instinctively that the disintegration of society begins with the death of idealism and convention. We know that for our society as a whole, and especially for the children, much depends upon the family unit remaining secure and respected.**' (Speech, Institution of Electrical Engineers, 26.7.82)

'**Our grandparents and parents brought us up without trendy theories and didn't make a bad job of it.**' (*Daily Mirror*, 25.5.78)

Documents were leaked to the press in 1983 from the Family Policy Group, a group consisting of Conservative MPs, Cabinet ministers, the Prime Minister and some of her advisers. The proposals advocated encouraging mothers to stay at home, and working out ways of *'encouraging families to reassume responsibilities taken on by the state; for example responsibility for the disabled, the elderly, unemployed 16-year-olds,'* and making parents responsible for *'some of the anti-social behaviour of their children'* (*Guardian*, 17.2.83). As Mrs Thatcher said:

'What is right for the family is right for Britain.' (*Sunday Express*, 29.6.75*)

'The nation is but an enlarged family.' (Speech from the pulpit of St Lawrence Jewry, 4.2.81)

Denis Thatcher says:

'Who could meet Margaret without being completely slain by her personality and intellectual brilliance?' (*The Times*, 5.10.70)

And, echoing his wife's philosophy;

'If I start something, by golly I mean to get to the top of the tree. I don't pretend I'm anything else but an honest-to-God right-winger – those are my views.' (Ibid.)

Denis has been known to say the wrong thing at the wrong time. On the occasion when Margaret publicly cradled a new-born calf, he said:

'If we're not careful, we'll have a dead calf on our hands.' (*Guardian*, 12.11.76)

Margaret remembers:

'I'm romantic enough to remember the details of my marriage. Of course I had my practical side and converted my wedding dress into a dinner dress and wore it for a long time afterwards.' (*Daily Mail*, 10.9.79)

'If you saw me at four o'clock in the morning with my make–up gone and running my hands through my hair you'd get a different picture.' (*Daily Express*, 13.8.80)

'I was just lucky with Denis. Absolutely marvellous. He's always encouraged me to use one's talents. Then we had a marvellous family. Everything just came right.' (BBC Radio 4, 30.2.81)

'Our home is both our base and our refuge. In the evenings we both just flop and talk.' (*News of the World*, 4.5.80)

'He has his rugger cronies and I have a circle of political friends. We have a life togther and a life apart and I think that's very important.' (*Daily Mail*, 3.5.80)

Carol says:

'*Mum and me aren't really close – but that's natural. I don't see much of her and when I do we say "Hi" and "Bye". I do admire her though, and I must say she looks amazing after four years in office … she'd probably say it's all thanks to being a square peg in a square hole.*' (*Woman*, 6.3.82)

Mark says:

'*I can never forget who she is and who I am. You'd be astonished at what this sometimes means.*' (*Daily Mirror*, 5.3.81)

Margaret says:

'Mark's made some mistakes but he's learned his lesson and he's learned fast enough. I'm very proud of him and he's always so thoughtful about me. When I have problems he's always the first to drop in and say, forget it, don't think about it.' (*Daily Express*, 13.3.80)

Mark and his mother have been together in the news over

'There are times when I've been desperately unhappy and disappointed … I knocked about a bit, as they say.' (*Observer*, 16.3.69)

'I stand here in my red chiffon gown, my face softly made up, my hair gently waved – The Iron Lady of the Western World?'
(*Sunday Telegraph*, 1.2.76)

'I am worried about my image. I'm going to change it ... I'm very aware that my image is important. I'm not at all pleased with the way I look on TV. I'm going to do something about it and the first thing is my hair. I'm going in for the unkempt look.' (*Daily Mail*, 4.5.76)

the Oman Affair – was Mrs Thatcher acting in her son's, as well as Britain's, interests when negotiating business for Britain in Oman in 1981?

Mark says:

'*I am responsible to three people on the planet. One of them is my mother, the second is the Almighty, and the third is me. My responsibility to her is as my mother, not as Prime Minister. To me, that is peripheral ... I played a very small part in a successful British contract.*' (*Sunday Times*, 12.2.84)

Mrs Thatcher says:

'**You want to know what my role is when I go on these tours to get jobs for Britain? I bat for Britain.**' (London Weekend Television, 15.1.84)

She despairs:

'**I hope we have not reached the stage when parents and their sons have to report everything to the authorities. If it comes to that, 1984 will be here.**' (*Hansard*, 23.1.84)

And:

'**I have answered question after question on this matter. There is nothing I can usefully add.**' (*Hansard*, 21.2.84)

His mother's last words on the subject:

'**The facts will be published – in 30 years time.**' (BBC Television, 9.4.84)

Anybody as much in the public eye as the Prime Minister can expect to make enemies and fans, to excite praise and criticism, to receive brickbats and bouquets. Margaret Thatcher is no exception. She invites criticism, but says:

'One has learned to take it, to cope with it. The more positive you become the more enemies you make.' (*Daily Telegraph*, 11.12.74)

And:

'I don't mind taking stick.' (*News of the World*, 20.9.81)

In early years the press was obsessed with her appearance: '*She is tall, dark, attractive, well built,*' wrote an admirer in the *London Evening Standard* in February 1949. He added, '*she is a woman who believes in Empire.*' The *Daily Express* gave her a page-three style eulogy: '*The handsome person of Mrs Thatcher, golden haired, blue eyed, blue dressed with an almost risky cut to the upper part of her costume. What an attractive government! What a fine figure! What an image!*' (17.7.62)

A reporter at the *Yorkshire Post* found her '*extremely easy on the eye*' (23.6.64) and the *Kent Messenger* evidently did too. Their reporter wrote: '*A beautiful mouth is her*

'I read very little myself. If there's a snide remark, I know it would put me off for two or three hours, stop me concentrating, so I don't look.' (*Daily Express*, 13.3.80)

most attractive feature only just in the lead from pretty blond hair and a clear pink and white complexion' (8.1.71). Jean Rook thought Mrs Thatcher was good enough to eat: *'The delicious pink and white Maggie can't help looking so like a marshmallow you want to toast her over her own glowing sincerity'* (*Daily Express*, 5.3.74).

As Mrs Thatcher rose to prominence in the Conservative Party the nation began to hear more of her voice. Not everyone liked it. The *Liverpool Daily Post* observed: *'She has a way of pronouncing the word "milk" which invests it with more gloom than any other in the language'* (21.2.72). In November 1976, Mrs Thatcher said, **'I can hear my voice getting high when I'm nervous and I try to make it lower.'**

But the voice still grates on some critics' ears. Angela Carter wrote: *'It is a voice from the past . . . it has adopted a form of "toff-speak" . . . the voice of a duchess in a farce or a pantomime dame . . . just what makes her sound so ridiculous are the barbarous echoes of past glories. It is a wonder that her perorations are not drowned by peels of laughter each time she opens her mouth and unpleasantly significant that they are not . . .'* She concludes that Mrs Thatcher's voice is like the one *'that broke in on your game with the little boy next door. "What are you doing? Put your knickers back on this instant!"'* (*New Statesman*, 3.6.83)

Admirers and critics alike are not short of comparison. Her son Mark noted: *'She has the constitution of an elephant'* (*Margaret Thatcher: A Profile*, Patricia Murray, W. H. Allen 1980). Novelist Salman Rushdie has called her *'Woadicea'*, and he said: *'What an achievement is hers. She has persuaded the nation that everything that goes wrong from unemployment to the crime rate is an Act of God or someone else's fault'* (*Guardian*, 23.5.83). Freddie Laker, a fan, encouraged her: *'Turn the screw until it bleeds, then turn it again . . . we want you forever. Please don't go away'*

(Finchley, 20.6.80). The Russians call Mrs Thatcher *'The Iron Maiden'*, a nickname she doesn't object to. A journalist from the French newspaper *Le Quotidien* went one further with the mineral imagery: *'She is a uranium lady giving off remarkable radiations. She smiled and felt she had literally to seduce her two* [male] *interviewers'* (11.3.80). The report went on to mention her *'saucy bewitching smiles, her sweet voice and pretty doll's face'*. A Sofrès poll conducted in France in May 1984 put Mrs Thatcher in third place as Most Unpopular World Leader, following Ayatollah Khomeini and Colonel Gaddafi.

Her own political circle is not entirely complimentary about the Thatcher style of leadership. When their comments get into print they are usually described as 'sources close to the Prime Minister'. *'She has palpably failed to do what we told her. She has fallen into the very trap she promised she never would. She has come under the influence of the layabouts and the landowners of the party,'* a person who counts himself as an ally told the *Sunday Times* (3.5.81). A member of her inner-circle said, *'She is a terribly lonely woman ... you have to love her, love her, love her'* (Ibid.). Another insider remembered: *'I'd made some bad mistake which caused her a lot of trouble, one of her staff said. I expected a real dressing down. Instead she gave me this look which meant: Nanny is not cross, she is just very, very sad'* (*Observer* 2.1.83).

Other Tory Wets are less cautious. Norman St John Stevas said: *'I am not through force of circumstance prejudiced in Mrs Thatcher's favour ... I would like the Government to be more concerned with the deprivations of the new poor and the unemployed and to be seen to do so'* (*Daily Express*, 4.12.83). Another unhappy and rejected man is Francis Pym, the first Foreign Secretary for 200 years to be sacked. In his book (*The Politics of Consent*, Hamish Hamilton 1984), he criticises Margaret Thatcher for her

'Always read. It is someone else's concentrated experience they have put down on paper.' (*Daily Telegraph*, 7.6.80)

'I think I probably had a natural talent for speaking anyway.' (*Liverpool Daily Post*, 3.5.67)

' [I am] leader of the pack. What's a leader for but to lead the pack? Of course they are behind me. If they were in front of me they would be leaders.' (London Weekend Television, 4.3.80)

'I had a horrid day yesterday having to tell people [that they had been re-shuffled out of the Cabinet] **and I could see the disappointment written in their faces. But I had to do it. I was a reluctant butcher.'** BBC Radio 1, 20.2.75)

'*tendency to think she is always right. In turn this leads her to believe that she can always do things better than other people which then encourages her to try to do everything herself. Central government now exercises direct control over more and more aspects of our lives and within the Government the Prime Minister exercises direct control over more and more departments.*'

In 1983 Mrs Thatcher won a place in the London *Standard's* competition for the World's Twelve Most Impressive Lips. She came under the 'stiffest upper' bracket. It's hardly surprising that her lip is stiff when old allies turn on her. Rupert Murdoch said: '*She's desperately tired, she's run out of puff, she's gone out of her mind*' (*Observer*, 4.12.83). Bill Deedes, editor of the *Daily Telegraph* said: '*Ironically, Mrs Thatcher has disappointed right-wing ideologues more than left-wing ideologues who never entertained extravagant hopes of her*' (*Daily Telegraph*, 9.3.84). He complained of a '*dull absence of class one crises*' and thought '*Government-issue banana skins aren't enough*' (Ibid).

Someone who has changed his tune is Brian Walden. He once said, in *Margaret Thatcher: A Profile*, by Patricia Murray: '*In years to come great novels and poems will be written about her. She will do more for the advance of women than all the events in history – she will truly liberate them.*' But in 1984 he wrote: '*Mrs Thatcher's best friends lack the guts to tell her that she is ceasing to be an effective politician. She was the master politican of our age. Right or wrong she stirred the voters as nobody has since the war. People loved her or hated her. Margaret the two-fisted battling radical is a sell-out at the box office. This couth, restrained, conventional Tory leader we now see hobnobbing with the fat cats is a crashing bore*' (*London Standard*, 13.3.84).

Of course Labour MPs have plenty to say. '*Margaret Thatcher is doing for monetarism what the Boston strangler did for door-to-door salesmen,*' said Denis Healey (*Guardian*, 15.2.79). Dennis Skinner said: '*She and her Government have created more havoc in Britain than the German High Command in the last war. Is it not time for the Westminster Ripper to join the unemployment trails, pack her bags and go?*' (*Hansard*, 26.1.82). Tam Dalyell, a tireless critic of the Government's role in the Falklands war, said: '*Of all the catastrophic slogans, none has led to greater grief than "My country right or wrong" and patriotism, pseudo-patriotism rather, has indeed been the refuge of our scoundrel Prime Minister*' (*Daily Mirror*, 14.11.83). And, referring to the sinking of the Belgrano, he said: '*Mrs Thatcher ordered Northwood* [Britain's Fleet headquarters] *to drown hundreds – it might have been more than 368 – of young men to escalate war and wreck peace*' (Ibid.).

Neil Kinnock asked: '*Is she still lecturing people without shoes on how to pull themselves up by their boot-straps?*' (*Hansard*, 1.12.83).

Eric Heffer keeps it brief: '*Stupid woman!*' (*Hansard*, 9.7.81). Tony Benn called her the '*most hated Prime Minister*' and continued: '*I am sorry to say this because I do not believe in personalities ... That woman cannot move around Britain without hundreds of police to protect her because of the damage she is doing to the lives and prospects of millions of British people*' (*Guardian*, 7.2.84).

Journalist Keith Waterhouse summed up Mrs Thatcher's reign:

'*Thatcherism is a self-addressed Valentine card or a hymn in the key of Me ... when they swot up on Thatcher the "ism" they will find nothing but a one-woman band playing "I Did It My Way"*' (*Daily Mirror*, 1.3.84).